"If you don't know the difference between a sweet potato and yam, you will now! Mary-Frances's globally inspired recipes si the versatility of this celebrated root vegetable. For the sweet potato lover, these easy-to-follow recipes have special rewards."

—ANA SORTUN, CHEF AT OLEANA, SOFRA, AND SARMA

"As a North Carolinian, I spend the full calendar year swimming in sweet potatoes, and Mary-Frances Heck's *Sweet Potatoes* is an informative and technique-loaded guide to these plentiful roots. The recipes combine the perspective of a well-traveled author's palate with a straightforward approach that's right at home in any kitchen. I am particularly taken with the recipes that allow the sweet potato to richly and economically stand in for meat (see the Sweet Potato "Big Macs" or Buffalo Sweet Potatoes). The sweet potato Cacio e Pepe challenged my favored classic approach as a pasta lover—and landed a spot in our home as a new favorite go-to."

—ASHLEY CHRISTENSEN, CHEF AND AUTHOR OF
Poole's: Recipes and Stories from a Modern Diner

SWEET
POTATOES

CLARKSON POTTER/PUBLISHERS

NEW YORK

ROASTED, LOADED, FRIED,

SWEET

AND MADE INTO PIE

POTATOES

MARY-FRANCES HECK

For the farmers and the cooks
who through history
have nourished others
with this humble root.

All rights reserved.
Published in the United States
by Clarkson Potter/Publishers,
an imprint of the Crown Publishing Group,
a division of Penguin Random House LLC,
New York.
crownpublishing.com
clarksonpotter.com

CLARKSON POTTER is a trademark
and POTTER with colophon is a registered
trademark of Penguin Random House LLC.

Library of Congress Cataloging-in-Publication Data is available upon request.

ISBN 978-0-451-49939-4
Ebook ISBN 978-0-451-49940-0

Printed in China

Cover and book design by Sonia Persad
Cover photography by Kristin Teig

10 9 8 7 6 5 4 3 2 1

First Edition

CONTENTS

INTRODUCTION

Sweet potatoes are a perfect food: delicious, a nutritional powerhouse, inexpensive, and endlessly adaptable. But despite their wholesomeness, sweet potatoes are often used as a vehicle for sugar and fat, hidden in the custard pies and marshmallow-topped casseroles served at Thanksgiving. This book pushes beyond those preparations, exploring both their sweet and savory sides with creative, doable recipes for everyday eating.

The wide-ranging recipes in these pages were created to inspire cooks to start eating and enjoying sweet potatoes like never before. The tantalizing, mellow sweetness of this root vegetable can be played up or down depending on how you prepare them. The many flesh colors—from purple to orange to creamy white (see page 14)—is an indicator of the moisture content of each variety, which helps determine the most suitable cooking method.

The next section, "A Sweet Potato Primer" (page 10), provides all the information you need to identify, select, store, and prepare sweet potatoes for recipes. The following chapter, "In the Rough" (page 16), breaks down sweet potato cookery into master methods. Exploring these basic recipes— roasting whole sweet potatoes and pieces, coal-roasting, boiling, steaming, and frying—builds a foundation for experimenting with sweet potatoes and discovering their versatility. The temptation to cook and serve sweet potatoes like starchy, tuberous, white potatoes leads many cooks to mash them or turn them into oven fries. But sweet potatoes have so much more potential! With these diverse cooking methods, you can transform this lowly root into dozens of new dishes.

The recipes in the rest of the book build upon these master cooking methods. Adaptable to dozens of flavor profiles and uses, the root vegetable appears in dishes that range from practically primitive (White Sweet Potatoes with Chimichurri, page 66) to rather refined (Sweet Potato Chocolate Babka, page 114). Many cultures count sweet potatoes as a staple food, and you'll find that the recipes here are influenced by cuisines near and far. *Canela*-laced Mexican candied sweet potatoes (page 127), a peanutty West African stew of braised sweet potato leaves (page 62), and Japanese sweet potato and shrimp fritters (page 48) are just a few of the dishes that draw on global influences. Seasonal ingredients, like asparagus and spring onions, are right at home with Sweet Potato Gnocchi (page 98), and summery Grilled Sweet Potatoes with Garlic-Maple Glaze (page 71) pair perfectly with any grilled meat. Sweet potatoes come alive paired with a larder's worth of ingredients: chiles, coconut, soy sauce and miso, chocolate, bacon, or berries. As you begin to explore all that sweet potatoes can do, try experimenting with the complementary flavors in the list on page 15.

When it comes to baking, you will be surprised by all that sweet potatoes can do, as they can take the place of sugar, flour, fat, and dairy in certain recipes. The "Breads and Baked Goods" (page 104) and "Sweets" (page 126) chapters explore this idea in depth. Many of these recipes call for Sweet Potato Puree (page 25) as an ingredient, which lends an earthy sweetness—along with moisture, starch, fiber, and nutrients—to baked goods. Sweet Potato Biscuits (page 105) use this puree in place of buttermilk, while Sweet Potato Milk Bread Dough (page 106) subs it in for part of the flour. There is something forgiving about baking with sweet potatoes; the results are guaranteed to be moist and decadent without inducing the hangover that follows indulging in sweets.

No marshmallows were harmed in the making of this book (well, maybe a dollop or two of marshmallow crème on the Sweet Potato Ice Cream, page 130). The sixty recipes in this book will inspire you to reach for this root vegetable every day—as a go-to for snacks, weeknight meals, and so much more. And while there are no recipes reserved exclusively for the holiday table, serving Black-Bottom Sweet Potato Pudding Pie (page 128) at Thanksgiving would make your grandma proud!

A SWEET POTATO PRIMER

Sweet potato roots, stems, and leaves are all edible, and the roots are considered a superfood—high in vitamins A and C, B-vitamins, potassium, and antioxidants; a good source of dietary fiber; and low on the glycemic scale.

Botanically speaking, the sweet potato (*Ipomoea batatas*) is the tuberous root vegetable of a vining plant related to the morning glory; their flowers look remarkably similar.

Though seemingly similar, sweet potatoes and potatoes (*Solanum tuberosum*) are genetically unrelated, and the edible parts of each plant are different. While sweet potato leaves are edible, solanaceous potato leaves are poisonous and should not be eaten. Sweet potatoes are tuberous roots, which are prone to holding fiber, sugar, vitamins, and minerals, whereas the edible part of the potato plant is called a stem tuber, an anatomical storage area that holds simple starch and sugar.

In some parts of the United States and Canada, sweet potatoes are referred to as *yams*. True yams encompass several species in the *Dioscorea* genus, and, while also a tuberous root vegetable, they are entirely unrelated to sweet potatoes. Yams have bumpy, tough, dark brown skin, with flesh that is starchy and not sweet. Confusion started in the 1930s, when Louisiana sweet potato growers, who favored an orange-fleshed variety, decided to market their sweet potatoes as "yams" in order to distinguish them from the sweet potato varieties grown in other states. Now, the US Department of Agriculture requires that all sweet potatoes are labeled as such, but the term *yam* is still used colloquially in many areas. Grocery stores frequently refer to sweet potatoes as yams on signage, so it is up to shoppers to know the qualities of sweet potatoes and be sure they are getting the correct vegetable. (That said, true yams are nearly impossible to find in most parts of the United States, so what you might think to be a yam is most likely a sweet potato.)

Sweet potatoes are eaten all over the world. Originally from Central America, prehistoric samples of sweet potatoes have been discovered in parts of Polynesia, where the word for sweet potato, *kumara,* is linguistically similar to the term used on the western coast of South America (provocatively suggesting that Columbus did not, in fact, discover the Americas). *Camote* is the term used in modern Mexico, Central America, and the Philippines. Columbus did, however, introduce the sweet potato to Europe, and he called it by one of its indigenous names, *batata*. Sweet potatoes were then cultivated in Europe, and the term *batata* was borrowed to refer to starchy potatoes, which were introduced to Europe a half century later.

SELECTION

Choose sweet potatoes that are firm and dry to the touch, with no soft spots or bruises. The skin should be uniformly colored, without marks or blemishes; a nick or bruise can quickly rot. The pointed ends should not be black, shriveled, or soft.

STORAGE

Try to purchase sweet potatoes no more than a week or two before you plan to use them. After harvest, sweet potatoes are stored in special cooling units that have controlled humidity. Once they are sent to the market, they slowly begin turning soft and losing the vibrancy of their flavor. When you get sweet potatoes home, remove them from the bag and store them in a cool, dry place, preferably in a basket or other container that allows air flow. Don't wash them until you are ready to use them.

CLEANING

Just before cooking, use a vegetable brush to scrub the sweet potatoes under cool running water. The skin holds many nutrients, so cleaning it well is an essential first step. Pat the sweet potatoes dry. If you are cooking the sweet potatoes whole by roasting or boiling, leave the skins on. If the potatoes will be diced, peel them with a vegetable peeler and discard the skins before dicing.

BUTCHERING

Cut sweet potatoes with a sharp, heavy knife on a large cutting board. Thin Japanese knives are made of brittle metal that can snap when cutting dense vegetables, so avoid using them on sweet potatoes. Begin by removing a thin slice from one broad side of the sweet potato so that it lies flat on the cutting board. Then continue cutting the sweet potato into the size and shape required for your recipe. Don't worry about perfect-looking pieces! It is more important that everything is about the same size so that they cook at the same rate.

SIZES

Sweet potatoes come in all sizes, ranging from a couple of ounces to over 2 pounds. Similar to the way shrimp are sold, it is helpful to use the number of sweet potatoes per pound to determine their size. Size is important because it affects cooking time—the bigger the sweet potato, the more time you need to cook it through.

BABY: 6 to 8 per pound, 2 to 3 ounces each

A pain to peel, these are best halved lengthwise and seared on a *plancha* (see page 65). Size is an indicator of maturity, and when they're in season, these small, moist babes will be tender in a flash. Seek them out at farmer's markets in the fall. Allow three or four baby sweet potatoes per person.

SMALL: 4 to 5 per pound, 3 to 4 ounces each

Their petite size makes these perfect for finger food or a kid's side dish. Try them in Twice-Baked Sweet Potatoes (page 42). Allow two or three small sweet potatoes per person.

MEDIUM: 2 to 3 per pound, 5 to 8 ounces each

Great for personal-size preparations, medium sweet potatoes are perfect for oven-roasting (see page 18) or for burying in coals (see page 20). They have a developed sweetness, tender skin, and toothsome texture that is not overly fibrous. One is enough for a serving.

LARGE: 1 to 1½ per pound, 12 to 16 ounces each

The most common size found in grocery stores and the most versatile, large sweet potatoes are handy for peeling and turning into any number of dishes. They roast evenly and have developed sugar content and structure. While large sweet potatoes may have an occasional stringy fiber running lengthwise through the flesh, it will rarely be noticeable if thoroughly cooked. One large sweet potato is enough for two servings.

EXTRA LARGE: Over 1 pound per sweet potato

These are ideal for chopping and cooking in a moist environment, such as boiling (see page 24) or steaming (see page 17). While they generally boast sweetness and moisture, extra-large sweet potatoes may also have more developed starch and fiber contents, which will become sweeter with moist cooking. One extra-large sweet potato is enough for two to four people.

Sweet potato leaves: Generally green, though also purple or white, young sweet potato leaves and stems are edible and high in vitamin K. They can be eaten raw or cooked, much like spinach, and have a mild, mineral flavor that is great in salads, stir-fries, and braises. Sweet potato leaves are widely eaten as a cooked green in Asia and West Africa.

TYPES

There are hundreds of varieties of sweet potatoes; keep an eye out for local ones at farmer's markets during the fall harvest season. Where important, each recipe in this book identifies the color and size of sweet potato required—and if neither is given, you can use whatever you like best. The following list should help you pick out the most common varieties found at grocery stores:

ORANGE FLESHED
(moist and soft when cooked)

Beauregard: Red to brown skin gives way to rich orange flesh. Moist and deeply sweet, with caramel and butterscotch notes, the Beauregard is the darling of Louisiana. The quintessential orange sweet potato, it is used in pies and casseroles throughout the South and is excellent roasted whole.

Garnet: Less sweet than Beauregard, though virtually identical looking, its dusty red skin masks deep-orange flesh. The lower sugar content means the Garnet's vegetal, pumpkin-like flavor shines through. The flesh is very moist and benefits from long, slow whole roasting or boiling and mashing.

Jewel: With tan to coppery-orange skin and deep-orange flesh, Jewel also looks similar to Garnet and Beauregard, making it hard to decipher among them unless they are stacked next to each other. Jewel's flavor is mildly sweet, earthy, and versatile. With medium-high water content and a firmer texture than Garnet or Beauregard, it is great for roasting whole or in pieces, or boiling and mashing for baked goods.

WHITE FLESHED
(dry and firm when cooked)

Hannah and O'Henry: White to yellow flesh lies beneath the dusty ivory to tan skin. Its sweet minerality shines with a buttery, silky texture when braised. Roasting will yield dry flesh with concentrated flavor, perfect for making gnocchi or drenching in sauce.

Japanese: The rusty-red to purplish-maroon skin gives way to cream-colored flesh that turns light yellow when cooked. Japanese sweet potatoes have a musky, rich sweetness like cashews or chestnuts. Their flesh can be quite dry and mealy when cooked hot and fast; instead, braise them in dashi or roast them whole, in the oven or on a bed of warm coals, to coax out and caramelize their natural sweetness.

PURPLE FLESHED
(dry and flaky when cooked)

Stokes Purple: A relatively new variety that is trademarked by a farmer in Stokes County, North Carolina, it has deep-purple flesh and skin. Brimming with anthocyanins, pigments with antioxidant properties, its dry flesh has a lightly sweet chestnut flavor when roasted and maintains its color surprisingly well when boiled whole. (Anthocyanins are water-soluble blue-colored compounds that tend to bleed when cooked in a moist environment.) Try mashing them with coconut milk.

Okinawan: Also known as Hawaiian, this is a white-skinned variety with purple-speckled to purple-saturated flesh. Bred in Japan and cultivated widely in Hawaii, Okinawan sweet potatoes have more antioxidants than blueberries. Generally small in size, they have tough skin and dry flesh. Boil them whole, then peel, slice, and dress or serve plain instead of another mild starch like rice or potatoes.

COMPLEMENTARY SEASONINGS AND INGREDIENTS

FRUITS: orange, lemon, lime, yuzu, peach, cherry, apricot, pineapple, coconut, mango, apple

VEGETABLES: chiles, onions, celery, carrots, mushrooms, corn, pole beans, peas, leafy greens, tomatoes

SPICES AND CONDIMENTS: cayenne, chili powder, cinnamon, nutmeg, cardamom, cumin, coriander, mustard, miso, soy sauce, chipotle in adobo, hot sauce, ketchup

HERBS AND AROMATICS: ginger, garlic, rosemary, cilantro, thyme, chives, scallions, oregano

SWEETENERS: brown sugar, honey, coconut sugar, molasses, chocolate, maple syrup

DAIRY AND FATS: butter, cream, whole milk, yogurt, coconut oil, sesame oil, olive oil, blue cheese, Parmesan, pecorino (sheep's milk cheese), goat cheese

PROTEINS: pork, chicken, turkey, beef, shrimp, fin fish, clams, scallops, lobster, black beans, butter beans, white beans, lentils

NUTS AND SEEDS: pecans, cashews, walnuts, almonds, peanuts, pepitas, sunflower seeds

SWEET POTATOES
♥
BUTTER

Sweet potatoes and butter are a match made in heaven. The fat from the butter helps your body to absorb the nutrients found in sweet potatoes, and the combinations below offer an extra hit of flavor. Each makes enough to dress 1 pound of boiled, roasted, or mashed sweet potatoes.

MISO BUTTER
Mash 2 tablespoons unsalted butter and 1 tablespoon red or white miso with a fork to form a paste.

MAPLE-WALNUT BUTTER
Mash 2 tablespoons chopped walnuts, 2 tablespoons unsalted butter, 1 tablespoon maple syrup, and a pinch of salt with a fork to form a chunky mixture.

OLD BAY BUTTER
Mash 2 tablespoons unsalted butter with 2 teaspoons Old Bay or Cajun seasoning with a fork until smooth.

IN THE ROUGH

STEAMED
SWEET POTATOES

Steaming sweet potatoes in batons or bite-size pieces is the best choice for when you want their sharp corners maintained and a moist result. This cooking method is the perfect way to prepare sweet potatoes for pickling (see page 40). Try cooled steamed sweet potatoes as crudités, or simply dress them with a little vinaigrette and they become an open-the-fridge-and-feed-yourself snack.

SERVES 4

2 pounds orange- or white-fleshed sweet potatoes

TIP: Make sure to cut the sweet potatoes into uniform pieces— cubes, batons, or slices—so they cook evenly and hold their shape.

1 In a large saucepan or pot fitted with a steamer basket, pour water to a depth of at least 2 inches. Cover, set over medium-high heat, and bring the water to a boil.

2 Meanwhile, peel the sweet potatoes and cut them into uniform pieces, less than 1 inch thick, in any shape you'd like.

3 When steam whistles from the saucepan, quickly and carefully (steam is hot!) add the pieces of sweet potato to the steamer basket. Re-cover the pot and steam the sweet potatoes until a cake tester or paring knife meets the tiniest, barely noticeable bit of resistance in the center of a couple of pieces, 10 to 15 minutes, depending on size and shape. They should be cooked through but retain enough structure not to fall apart. Transfer the sweet potatoes to a plate or shallow dish and let cool.

OVEN-ROASTED
SWEET POTATOES

Roasting sweet potatoes may seem like a no-brainer, but, as George Washington Carver wisely wrote, "A sweet potato cooked quickly is not well cooked. Time is an essential element. Twenty minutes may serve to bake a sweet potato so that a hungry man can eat it, but if the flavor is an object, it should be kept in the oven for an hour."

Starting the sweet potatoes in a cool oven, whenever possible, warms the flesh slowly and evenly without turning the skin into inedible jerky. The sweet potatoes may become tender before they are fully delicious; look for caramelized juice bubbling from the ends of the sweet potatoes and collapsed skin.

SERVES 4

2 pounds orange-fleshed sweet potatoes, scrubbed

Unsalted butter, for serving (optional)

Kosher or flaky sea salt, for serving (optional)

TIPS: When roasting at high altitude, root vegetables can take up to twice as long to become tender, so plan accordingly.

When roasting whole sweet potatoes, always line the baking sheet or dish with foil or parchment, as the caramelized sweet potato juices are difficult to clean off the pan.

1 Line a rimmed baking sheet with aluminum foil or parchment paper. Use a fork to prick the sweet potatoes in several places; then arrange the sweet potatoes in a single layer on the baking sheet. Place the baking sheet on the middle rack of the oven and heat the oven to 350°F.

2 Bake the sweet potatoes until their juices bubble like lava from the volcanic ends and pricked skin, caramelizing into a dark pumice, and the skin has softened, dried out, and collapsed onto the flesh, an hour, give or take, depending on the weight and width of your sweet potatoes. It may take up to 2 hours for very large ones weighing more than 1 pound. Remove the sweet potatoes from the oven and let them rest until their juices no longer flow, about 5 minutes. Serve hot with butter and salt, if desired.

COAL-ROASTED
SWEET POTATOES

This is perhaps the first way humans cooked sweet potatoes nearly ten thousand years ago. Coal-roasting sweet potatoes yields fluffy, smoky flesh. When the skins are cracked open, they are the perfect vehicle for Sambal Butter (page 73) or a dollop of *skyr* or crème fraîche. Make sure to brush away the ashes, leaving bits of crusty, charred skin for textural contrast. As the name implies, you will need a hardwood or charcoal fire, burned down to embers, for this recipe. A pair of long metal tongs and a metal shovel of sorts, preferably a wok spatula with a wooden handle, are essential tools and are available for a couple of bucks at kitchen supply stores.

SERVES 4

4 medium or large orange-, white-, or purple-fleshed sweet potatoes (2 to 3 pounds)

1 Build a large wood fire in a pit or a charcoal fire in a kettle grill. (If using a grill, remove the cooking grate and set it aside while positioning the sweet potatoes; the grate may be returned and used for cooking other items once the sweet potatoes are buried.) If desired, individually wrap each sweet potato in a sheet of foil.

2 When the flames from the fire subside and the coals are covered in a thick layer of gray ash, after about 15 minutes, arrange half of the coals in an even bed. Nestle the sweet potatoes into the coals and use the wok spatula to scoop the remaining embers over and around the sweet potatoes to completely bury them. (It may seem counterintuitive, but any area not smothered in coals is more likely to flare up and burn an inedible charred spot on the sweet potato.) Cook the sweet potatoes without disturbing them for about 20 minutes.

3 Use the wok spatula to scrape away the embers. Insert a cake tester or paring knife into one of the sweet potatoes to see how much of the

flesh has softened; likely the bottom part of the sweet potato that was resting on the bed of coals will be more cooked and charred than the top. Use tongs to turn the sweet potatoes over and bury them again in embers. Cook until the sweet potatoes are tender throughout and caramel bubbles from cracks in the skin, 20 to 40 more minutes, depending on size. Carefully lift them from the coals and set them on a heatproof plate. Allow any sparks on the skins to burn out, and then use a clean dish towel or pastry brush to wipe away any ashes or burned skin. Transfer the whole cleaned sweet potatoes to serving plates or crack them into bite-size pieces with a bit of char on each.

VARIATIONS

Twice Coal-Roasted Sweet Potatoes

1 Set a cleaned coal-roasted sweet potato on a 12-inch-square sheet of foil. Cut a lengthwise slit halfway through the sweet potato, as for a baked potato, and push the ends toward one another to fluff the flesh.

2 Stuff the sweet potato with a pat of unsalted butter, a shake of cayenne, a tablespoon of chopped scallions, and a tablespoon of grated melty cheese like Jack or Cheddar.

3 Press the sweet potato closed and crimp the foil over the sweet potato to seal. Return to the coals until melted and hot, about 5 minutes.

Chocolate-Cinnamon-Sugar Sweet Potatoes

1 Cut the sweet potato open and push the ends toward one another to fluff the flesh. Top the flesh with a pat of unsalted butter, 1 tablespoon brown sugar, 1 tablespoon chocolate chips, and ¼ teaspoon ground cinnamon.

2 Press the sweet potato closed and crimp the foil over the sweet potatoes to seal. Return to the coals until melted and hot, about 5 minutes.

BOILED
SWEET POTATOES

Boiling sweet potatoes yields evenly cooked, moist chunks perfect for adding to soups or dressing as for potato salad. Be sure to boil different varieties separately. Each will take a different amount of time to become tender, and purple sweet potatoes will bleed their color into the water, dyeing the other sweet potatoes.

SERVES 4

2 pounds orange-, white-, or purple-fleshed sweet potatoes

Kosher salt (optional)

Peel the sweet potatoes and cut them into 1-inch chunks. Put the sweet potatoes in a large saucepan and cover with cool water by 1 inch. Season lightly with salt if making a savory preparation. Set the pan over medium-high heat and bring to a rapid boil. Reduce the heat to medium-low to maintain a vigorous simmer. Cook the sweet potatoes until a paring knife inserted into a few different chunks meets no resistance, 12 to 15 minutes from when they first came to a boil. Drain the sweet potatoes and discard the cooking water.

TIP: Since sweet potatoes don't require as much salt as starchy white potatoes, it is best to season the sweet potatoes *after* boiling, or use just a little salt in the water.

SWEET POTATO
PUREE

This puree is part of a well-stocked freezer, as it can be adapted endlessly in many recipes or eaten as a quick, nukeable side dish. By cooking the sweet potatoes without salt, you end up with a versatile base ingredient that can be dressed simply with butter and salt, or added to many of the baked goods and sweets found in the last two chapters. It's also delicious seasoned with one of the flavored butters on page 15.

MAKES ABOUT 2 CUPS

1½ pounds orange-fleshed sweet potatoes

1 Peel the sweet potatoes and cut them into 1-inch cubes. Put the sweet potatoes in a large saucepan and add cool water to cover by 1 inch. Set the pan over medium-high heat and bring to a boil. Reduce the heat to low to maintain a gentle simmer and cook until the sweet potatoes are fully tender about 15 minutes. Drain the sweet potatoes, reserving the cooking liquid.

2 For a perfectly smooth puree, first pass the sweet potatoes through a food mill or press them through a potato ricer, discarding any pulpy, stringy flesh that remains. Give the milled sweet potatoes a good stir with a spoon, and add a tablespoon or two of cooking liquid if the puree seems dry or tacky. For a coarser puree, simply mash the sweet potatoes with the back of a fork or a potato masher. They will collapse into a relatively smooth mass that should not require additional liquid to remain moist. To store, let the puree cool and then refrigerate it in an airtight container for up to 3 days. To freeze, place cupfuls of puree in sandwich-size plastic zip-top bags, flatten the bags as you seal them, and stack them in the freezer.

TIP: While boiling sweet potatoes for puree provides the most consistent texture and flavor, you can cook them in the microwave for use in baked goods. Prick the skin with a fork and microwave in 4-minute intervals, flipping the sweet potatoes between intervals. The total cook time will depend on the size and moisture content of the sweet potatoes, usually 8 to 12 minutes.

SWEET POTATO FRIES

Making really good sweet potato fries has been one of the great recipe challenges of the twenty-first century. Whether they are roasted or deep fried, a few minutes later, they're limp. The very reason that sweet potatoes are considered healthier than white potatoes—they contain less simple starch, which is metabolized as sugar—is the root of why sweet potato fries don't get crispy on the outside and fluffy on the inside.

When white potatoes are "french fried," they are first cooked at a low temperature to cook the potato and gel the outer layer of starch on its surfaces, then cooked again at a higher temperature to crisp the gelled starch. The result is a crisp, dry outside encasing a moist inside. To approximate this gelled starch coating for sweet potatoes, processed food companies, chefs, and even NASA have conducted tons of tests. Experimental steps include washing, drying, blanching, alkalinizing, dehydrating, freezing, dredging, and battering the poor spuds before their eventual trip(s) through hot oil. After testing a dozen methods and studying the results, the following two recipes evolved.

Sweet potato fries made The Hard Way (page 28) are deep fried and require a few steps that will dirty some dishes, but are worth it. First, a dusting of baking soda and cornstarch clings to the fries and begins to rough up and gelatinize the surface starch. Then, freezing them buys the outside of the fries a little longer to crisp in the oil before the inside become soft. Dipping the frozen fries in a slurry adds a layer of dissolved starch that begins to gel as soon as it hits the oil. These essential steps yield sweet potatoes worthy of the term *fry*.

Making them The Easy Way (page 29) distills the oven-fry method to its most essential steps: cutting the sweet potatoes uniformly so they cook evenly, oiling and seasoning them aggressively, then roasting them in a hot oven until crisp.

SWEET POTATO FRIES
THE HARD WAY

SERVES 4

2 pounds large orange-fleshed sweet potatoes

1 teaspoon baking soda

1 cup plus 2 tablespoons cornstarch

Peanut oil, for frying

1 cup club soda or water

Kosher or fine sea salt

1 Line a baking sheet with parchment paper and make enough room in the freezer for said baking sheet.

2 Peel the sweet potatoes, if desired, and cut them lengthwise into ¼-inch-thick batons (fry shapes). Place them in a bowl with the baking soda and 2 tablespoons cornstarch, and toss. Arrange the sweet potatoes on the baking sheet in a single layer, making sure they are not touching. Freeze them until rock hard, at least 3 hours. If making fries later, transfer to a gallon-size zip-top freezer bag; they will keep frozen for up to 2 weeks.

3 Pour the oil into a large, heavy pot, preferably a Dutch oven, that's fitted with a deep-fry thermometer to a depth of 2 inches. Set the pot over medium heat and begin gently warming the oil to 375°F.

4 In a large bowl, whisk together the remaining 1 cup cornstarch and the club soda. Stack several layers of brown paper on a baking sheet.

5 When the oil reaches 375°F, drop a handful of sweet potatoes into the cornstarch mixture and coat evenly. Lift them from the bowl, letting any excess drip into the bowl, and carefully add them to the oil. Fry, stirring with a spider so they do not stick to the bottom of the pot, until deep golden brown and cooked through, about 8 minutes. Using the spider, transfer the fries to the brown paper to drain. Immediately season with salt. Repeat with the remaining sweet potatoes, returning the oil to 375°F between batches.

SWEET POTATO FRIES
THE EASY WAY

SERVES 4

2 pounds orange-fleshed sweet potatoes

2 tablespoons canola oil, olive oil, or melted unsalted butter

1½ teaspoons kosher or fine sea salt

TIP: While both recipes only call for salt, try adding a teaspoon or two of any of your favorite seasonings. Got some herbes de Provence? Toss 'em in there. Spanish paprika? Definitely. Za'atar, curry powder, Mrs. Dash, Old Bay, or Tony Chachere's? Yes, please.

1 Preheat the oven to 375°F. Line a rimmed baking sheet with parchment paper.

2 Peel the sweet potatoes, if desired, and cut them into slabs, batons, wedges, coins, half-moons, or cubes. They can be any size, really, as long as they are not less than ¼ inch and not more than 1 inch thick. Place them in a large bowl and drizzle with the oil. Season with salt and your choice of spices, if using, and toss to coat. (Use about 1½ teaspoons salt if you're not using additional seasoning; adjust salt content depending on your preferred spice mix.) Dump the sweet potatoes onto the prepared baking sheet, scraping out any seasoning or fat clinging to the bowl, and arrange them in a single layer.

3 Roast, turning once if their bottoms darken quickly, until tender and browned, 15 to 25 minutes, depending on size.

SWEET POTATO
CHIPS

Bagged, store-bought sweet potato chips lose their character when left on a shelf for months. This recipe has several steps, but none of them is hard, and the result is far superior to any chip you can buy. Soaked in water to wash away their starch, the chips maintain the very essence of sweet potato flavor without becoming soggy or greasy. Set aside your fear of frying, because it's fun to do when you are well equipped; see Essentials for Frying (page 32) for how to set yourself up for success.

SERVES 4

1 pound medium or large orange-fleshed sweet potatoes, scrubbed

Neutral oil, such as canola, grapeseed, or peanut, for frying

Kosher or fine sea salt

1 Trim off one end of each sweet potato. Using a mandoline, shave thin (1/16 inch or so) round slices from the sweet potatoes into a large bowl. Fill the bowl with cold water, submerging the slices. Gently swish them around and then pour off the starchy water. Refill the bowl with cold water, cover with plastic wrap, and refrigerate for at least 1 hour and up to 24 (the longer they soak, the crisper the chips will be).

2 When ready to fry the chips, pour the oil into a large, heavy pot to a depth of 2 inches. Arrange several layers of brown paper or paper towels on a large rimmed baking sheet. Have a spider handy. Lift the sweet potatoes from the bowl and put them into a salad spinner. Discard the starchy water. Spin the sweet potato slices, discarding the water that collects in the spinner, until they are very dry, three or four good spins.

3 Submerge a thermometer probe in the oil and set the pot over medium heat. When the oil reaches 275°F, add a large handful of

recipe continues

sweet potatoes and stand back. When the steam cloud subsides, after 10 or so seconds, use the spider to push the chips down into the oil, turning them as they cook. Continue turning them to fry evenly until the bubbling subsides and the chips turn light golden brown, about 2 minutes.

4 Lift them from the oil using the spider, shake off any excess oil, and put them on the brown paper to drain. Immediately season with salt. When the oil returns to 275°F, continue frying in batches.

5 Transfer the chips to a bowl and serve warm, or let cool and store in a brown-paper-lined airtight container for up to 1 day.

ESSENTIALS FOR FRYING

Frying requires a few low-tech pieces of equipment—and one key ingredient—that are great for many tasks. Consider investing a few bucks in the following tools.

DUTCH OVEN: Also known as a large, heavy pot, nothing beats the ones cast by Le Creuset (or their warranty), but other models will do nicely, too. Choose one with a 7- to 8-quart capacity for deep-frying.

SALAD SPINNER: I bought my first salad spinner when I was almost thirty years old. I had been cooking professionally for over a decade and finally broke down and bought one for $4 at Ikea. After resisting what I thought was unnecessary kitchen equipment for so long, I starting using that salad spinner every day for drying tender herbs, blanched greens, and vegetables headed for the fryer.

SPIDER: Available at many Asian grocery stores or kitchen supply stores, this simple tool resembles a handled spider web. It's good for quickly catching anything floating around in hot oil.

DIGITAL THERMOMETER: Don't spend more than $20 on a kitchen thermometer. As long as the packaging has "NSF" printed on it (which means it's certified), it will be reliable. If you buy only one thermometer, let it be a digital probe meat thermometer that reads to at least 400°F, which works for temping meat, most candies, and fried foods.

BROWN PAPER BAGS: This is the best thing you can use to drain fried food. The paper absorbs grease without drawing moisture from the air or from inside the food, which paper towels tend to do. I like to cut out the narrow sides from the bags and turn them inside out so the "clean" inside of the bag is in contact with the cooked food.

NEUTRAL OIL: A fancy term for the plainest of oils, neutral oil is pale in color, lacking in flavor, and can take an awful lot of heat before it starts to smoke. Canola, grapeseed, and peanut oils are all great choices.

BIG BITES AND SMALL PLATES

BUFFALO
SWEET POTATOES

Roasted with lots of garlic, smothered in sauce, and topped with blue cheese and celery, these sweet potatoes are so good that you'll never want wings again. Put out a platter of these, and they'll be gone before the game starts.

SERVES 4

2 large sweet potatoes (about 2 pounds)

1 head of garlic, cloves separated

1 tablespoon neutral oil, such as canola or grapeseed

Kosher salt

4 tablespoons (½ stick) unsalted butter

½ teaspoon freshly ground black pepper

⅛ teaspoon cayenne pepper

½ cup Frank's Red Hot or Texas Pete hot sauce

2 celery ribs, thinly sliced on an angle

¼ cup crumbled blue cheese

1 Preheat the oven to 400°F. Line a rimmed baking sheet with parchment paper.

2 Peel and cut the sweet potatoes into 1-inch-thick, two-bite rounds or half-moons. Toss them in a bowl with the garlic cloves, oil, and a big pinch of salt. Arrange the sweet potatoes and garlic in a single layer on the prepared baking sheet, and roast until tender and browned, about 30 minutes.

3 Meanwhile, melt the butter in a small saucepan over medium heat (or in a bowl in the microwave). Stir in the black pepper, cayenne, and ½ teaspoon salt. Remove the pan from the heat and let sit for 15 minutes so the spices can bloom (release their flavor into the butter). Armed with a whisk, begin dashing the hot sauce into the butter, whisking until you have incorporated all the hot sauce and formed a creamy emulsion. This sauce is good on everything and will keep in the fridge for up to 1 month.

4 When the sweet potatoes are done roasting, pop the roasted garlic cloves from their skins back onto the pan, discarding the skins. Toss or drizzle the sweet potatoes with the buffalo sauce and arrange them on a large plate. Top with the celery slices and crumbled blue cheese.

JIAO YEN "SALT AND PEPPER"
SWEET POTATOES

Here, sweet potatoes are given the "salt and pepper" treatment, a Chinese preparation that's usually reserved for shrimp or pork. The potatoes are dusted in cornstarch, fried until tender and golden, then tossed with a Sichuan pepper–salt mixture and aromatics. The pepper-salt can also be used as a seasoning for roast chicken or raw veggies. See Essentials for Frying (page 32) for equipment and helpful tips about frying.

SERVES 4

2 teaspoons coarse sea salt

1 teaspoon Sichuan peppercorns

2 large white- or purple-fleshed sweet potatoes (about 2 pounds), peeled and cut into ½-inch-thick rounds or half-moons

¼ cup cornstarch

Neutral oil, such as canola or grapeseed, for frying

2 scallions (white and green parts), cut into ½-inch slices

2 fresh hot red chiles, cut into rings

1 Place the salt in a large skillet set over medium-low heat. Shake the skillet, toasting the salt until it starts to turn yellow, about 5 minutes. Dump the salt onto a plate and add the peppercorns to the skillet. Toast until fragrant and a wisp of smoke rises from them, about 20 seconds. Transfer to the plate with the salt and let cool. Buzz the salt and peppercorns in a spice grinder, or pound in a mortar and pestle, until finely ground.

2 In a gallon-size plastic zip-top bag, toss the sweet potatoes with the cornstarch to coat them evenly. Use your hands to lift the sweet potatoes from the bag (reserve the bag of corn starch) and place them in a sieve or colander. Shake off any excess cornstarch.

3 In a large, heavy pot or wok, fitted with a deep-fry thermometer, heat 2 inches of oil to about 325°F. Lay several layers of brown paper on a rimmed baking sheet and have a spider handy.

4 Working in batches of 7 or 8 pieces, fry the sweet potatoes until they are tender and golden, moderating the heat as necessary to hover between 325°F and 350°F, 8 to 10 minutes. Using the spider, lift the sweet potatoes from the oil and put them on the paper to drain. Immediately season with a generous sprinkle of the pepper-salt mixture. Repeat with the remaining sweet potatoes until they are all cooked.

5 Toss the scallions and chiles in the bag of cornstarch to coat them, shaking off any excess in the sieve, then add them to the oil. Flash-fry them for 10 to 20 seconds, until they are golden but not overcooked. Transfer to the paper-lined rimmed baking sheet and season everything once again with the remaining pepper-salt. Toss to coat and divide them among serving dishes.

CROSTINI WITH SPECK

A good bottle of sherry costs less than a good bottle of wine, so that should be reason enough to pair these little toasts with glasses of dry amontillado. The bit of work required at the front end means that, when it's time to serve, these toasts come together in a snap. Use any leftover sweet potato–apple butter to sauce pork chops, finish pasta, or serve on a cheese board.

MAKES 32 CROSTINI

SWEET POTATO–APPLE BUTTER

2 pounds orange-fleshed sweet potatoes, peeled and diced

4 cups apple cider

¾ cup packed light brown sugar

½ teaspoon kosher salt

32 baguette slices, ½ inch thick

16 slices speck, prosciutto, or country ham, torn in half

Freshly ground black pepper

1 **Make the sweet potato–apple butter:** In a large, heavy pot or Dutch oven, combine the sweet potatoes, cider, brown sugar, and salt.

2 Set the pot over medium heat and bring to a simmer. Moderate the heat as needed to maintain a vigorous simmer and cook, stirring occasionally to make sure the sweet potatoes do not scorch, until they are very soft, about 30 minutes.

3 Meanwhile, preheat the oven to 300°F.

4 Mash the mixture with a potato masher for a coarser butter or puree it with an immersion blender for smoother results. Scrape down the sides of the pot with a rubber spatula. Slide the pot into the oven and bake, stirring every 30 minutes, until the mixture is very thick and glossy, 1½ to 2 hours. Let cool, then transfer to an airtight container. (There will be about 4 cups.) The sweet potato–apple butter will keep, covered and refrigerated, for 1 month.

5 When ready to serve, toast the baguette slices. Smear each with sweet potato–apple butter. Top with some speck and freshly ground black pepper.

VEGGIE TEMAKI

MAKES 8 ROLLS

1 pound orange-fleshed sweet potatoes, peeled and cut into ½ × 2-inch batons

½ cup rice vinegar

¼ cup sugar

1 teaspoon kosher salt

8 half sheets nori (about 8 × 4 inches each)

2 cups warm cooked short-grain rice

Sesame seeds

2 cups mixed tender herb leaves, like shiso, mint, basil, and/or cilantro

4 scallions (green parts only), cut into 2-inch pieces

1 cucumber, peeled, seeded, and cut into ¼ × 2-inch batons

1 avocado, peeled, pitted, and thinly sliced

2 to 3 tablespoons spicy mayo (store-bought or a reliable mix of 3 parts mayo and 1 part Sriracha sauce)

Soy sauce, for dipping

Temaki is sushi's easy-rolling cousin. You don't need a special mat or any practice to make these rolls look delicious. Serve the nori, rice, pickled sweet potatoes, and fillings family-style—as you would for taco night—and let everyone pick and choose their favorite fillings.

1 Prepare the sweet potatoes according to the Steamed Sweet Potatoes recipe, page 17. Remove and arrange the steamed batons in a single or double layer in an 8-inch square or similar shallow baking dish.

2 In a small bowl, stir together the rice vinegar, sugar, salt, and ½ cup of water until the sugar is dissolved. Pour the pickling liquid over the warm sweet potatoes and let cool. Cover and refrigerate for at least 1 hour and up to 3 days.

3 When ready to assemble the temaki, gather all of the fillings at a workstation. Working with one sheet of nori at a time, wave the nori over an open flame or place it in a hot skillet until it is lightly crisped, 2 to 3 seconds. Place the sheet of toasted nori on a dry work surface and spread about ¼ cup of warm rice over half of the nori sheet. Sprinkle with some sesame seeds and then arrange several leaves of herbs over the rice. Line up 3 or 4 batons of sweet potato pickle diagonally over the herbs and rice, followed by a few pieces of scallion, cucumber, and avocado. Top with a little spicy mayo. Bring the far corner of nori and rice up and over the vegetables, forming a triangle. Continue rolling the nori around the fillings until you have a cone-shaped temaki. Repeat with the remaining ingredients until you have 8 rolls. Serve immediately with soy sauce for dipping.

TIP: Don't overload your temaki!

TWICE-BAKED
SWEET POTATOES

SERVES 4 TO 6

2 pounds small or medium sweet potatoes (about 6 to 8)

1 tablespoon neutral oil, such as canola or grapeseed

Kosher salt

1 chipotle chile from a can of chipotles in adobo sauce, chopped

2 tablespoons adobo sauce from the canned chipotles, plus more as needed

1½ cups drained cooked or canned black beans

1 cup grated Cheddar or Monterey Jack cheese

½ cup sour cream

½ cup chopped scallions (white and green parts)

1 avocado, peeled, pitted, and diced

Sliced pickled jalapeños (optional)

Somewhere between a healthy version of a potato skin and a loaded platter of nachos lie these baby sweet potatoes. Mashed with spicy chipotle, the soul mate of the sweet potato, their sweet, earthy flesh leans savory with the addition of the piquant, smoky chiles. And, the combination of sweet potatoes and black beans provides a protein-packed vegetarian snack or main course.

1 Preheat the oven to 350°F. Line a rimmed baking sheet with parchment paper.

2 Slice the sweet potatoes lengthwise in half, rub with the oil, and season with salt. Arrange them, cut-side down, on the prepared baking sheet and roast until tender and the kitchen smells like caramel, about 25 minutes. Set the sweet potatoes aside to cool; increase the oven temperature to 375°F.

3 When the sweet potatoes are cool enough to handle, scoop out most of the flesh from each skin, leaving a ¼-inch shell intact to help the skins maintain structure. Place the flesh in a bowl and use a fork to mash it with the chopped chipotle and adobo sauce. Fold in the beans and season to taste with salt and another spoonful of adobo sauce, if you like it spicy.

4 Line up the sweet potato skins and choose the 12 prettiest and most structurally sound; scrape out the remaining skins, add the flesh to the black bean mixture, and discard the skins. Place the 12 showcase skins on a fresh piece of parchment on the baking sheet. Divide the black

bean mixture evenly among them. Pile a big pinch of cheese on top of each and return the stuffed sweet potatoes to the oven. Roast until the filling is hot and the cheese is melted and bubbly, about 10 minutes.

5 Remove the stuffed sweet potatoes from the oven, transfer to a big platter, and anoint each with blobs of sour cream. Scatter with the scallions and avocado. Crown with jalapeño slices, if desired, and serve.

HOT PEPPER LABNE WITH
SWEET POTATO WEDGES

This dish is at once hot and cool, spicy and sweet, crispy and creamy. It is the wizardry of Cara Chigazola, who devised this dish while chef de cuisine at Ana Sortun's fabulous Mediterranean restaurant, Oleana, in Cambridge, Massachusetts. The genius method for making sweet potato wedges has two steps: first roast them dry, without any oil or seasoning, to slightly dehydrate the sweet potato and concentrate its sugar; then fry them up crisp. Their rich, earthy sweetness pairs perfectly with the unctuous, spicy *labne,* a thick, yogurt-like cheese from the Levant.

SERVES 4

HOT PEPPER LABNE

2 Hungarian hot wax or jalapeño peppers

3 tablespoons olive oil

1 tablespoon fresh lemon juice

1 teaspoon finely chopped garlic

1 cup labne or full-fat Greek yogurt

Kosher salt

2 pounds medium or large white- or orange-fleshed sweet potatoes (about 3 or 4), scrubbed

Neutral oil, such as canola or grapeseed, for frying

Kosher salt

Kibbeh Spice (recipe follows)

1 Preheat the oven to 350°F.

2 **Make the hot pepper labne:** Place the peppers in a shallow roasting dish and drizzle with 1 tablespoon of the oil. Roll them around to coat them evenly in the oil, and then roast until the skins are blistered, about 15 minutes. Let cool. When the peppers are cool enough to handle, carefully peel away the skins and remove the stems and seeds. Finely chop the roasted peppers.

3 In a medium bowl, combine the lemon juice and garlic. Let stand for 10 minutes to "cook" the garlic, muting its pungency with the fresh acid of the lemon. Whisk in the chopped peppers, remaining 2 tablespoons olive oil, and labne. Season with salt to taste. The labne can be made up to 3 days ahead. Cover and chill until ready to use.

recipe continues

TIP: Make the Hot Pepper Labne at least 2 hours before serving so the flavors have time to meld.

4 Cut the sweet potatoes lengthwise into 1-inch-wide wedges, like large skin-on steak fries. Place them on a parchment-lined rimmed baking sheet and roast until cooked through and dry on the surface but not crisp, about 30 minutes. The sweet potatoes can be prepared up to 1 hour before frying; keep at room temperature.

5 In a large, heavy pot or Dutch oven fitted with a frying thermometer, pour in the neutral oil to a depth of 2 inches. Heat the oil over medium heat to 350°F. Line a rimmed baking sheet with brown paper or paper towels. Have a spider handy.

6 Fry the roasted sweet potatoes in batches of 6 to 8 until golden brown and crispy, about 4 minutes per batch. Use the spider to lift the fries from the oil and set on the brown paper to drain. Immediately season the hot fries with salt and a generous sprinkle of kibbeh spice.

7 Serve the fries with the hot pepper labne for dipping.

KIBBEH SPICE
MAKES ¼ CUP

This recipe makes a little more than you need for the Hot Pepper Labne with Sweet Potato Wedges, but once you taste it, you'll have no trouble finding other uses for it.

1 tablespoon ground cumin

1½ teaspoons dried red chile flakes

1 tablespoon sweet paprika

1 tablespoon garlic powder

1½ teaspoons dried parsley

Combine the cumin, chile flakes, paprika, garlic powder, and parsley in an airtight container and shake to combine. Cover and store at room temperature for up to 1 week.

SWEET POTATO
CHIPS CON VALENTINA

This is barely a recipe, but it is so good! And unless you've tried it from a street cart in Mexico, it might be a surprising combination. The sweet, crunchy chips get spiced up—and I dare say, pleasantly soggy—from the Valentina hot sauce and lime. It's a one-two pucker-punch that keeps you reaching into the bowl for another.

SERVES 2

4 cups sweet potato chips, homemade (page 30) or store-bought

Kosher or fine sea salt (optional)

Valentina hot sauce

½ lime, cut into wedges

Place the sweet potato chips in a large bowl and season with salt (if they haven't already been salted). Douse with a dozen dashes or so of Valentina. Toss with a big spoon to coat the chips with the hot sauce, and then squeeze a couple of lime wedges over the top. Turn on your favorite telenovela, and munch!

KAKIAGE

Kakiage is casual tempura; instead of painstakingly dipping each item in a delicate batter and frying it individually, thinly sliced ingredients are folded into a bowl of batter. Spooned into hot oil, they become light and crispy fritters. For beautiful results, use several colors of small sweet potatoes.

MAKES TWENTY 2-INCH FRITTERS

12 ounces small sweet potatoes, preferably several different colors (about 3 sweet potatoes), peeled

1 leek (white part only), cut into ⅛-inch-thick half-moons

1 serrano chile or jalapeño pepper, sliced

8 ounces peeled shrimp, cut into ½-inch pieces

1½ teaspoons kosher salt

1 cup cake flour

2 tablespoons cornstarch

¾ cup ice water, plus more as needed

Neutral oil, such as canola or grapeseed, for frying

Soy Dipping Sauce (recipe follows)

1 To julienne the sweet potatoes, cut a sliver from one broad side of each sweet potato. Steady it on the flat side and begin slicing it as evenly as possible into very thin (about ⅛-inch) planks; it is more important that they be uniformly thin than any exact thickness. Stack the planks up, then slice them lengthwise into matchstick-size pieces. If necessary, cut them crosswise into 1-inch lengths.

2 Combine the sweet potatoes, leek, serrano, and shrimp in a large bowl and season with the salt. Add 1 to 2 tablespoons of the cake flour and toss; the flour will help the batter adhere to the ingredients.

3 In a separate medium bowl, whisk together the remaining cake flour, the cornstarch, and ¾ cup ice water. Add more water, a tablespoon at a time, if needed to make the batter smooth and fall like a ribbon. Pour the batter over the vegetables and shrimp, and fold until combined. The kakiage mixture should look like creamy, overdressed coleslaw.

4 Arrange several layers of brown paper or paper towels on a large rimmed baking sheet. In a large, heavy pot fitted with a deep-fry thermometer, heat 2 inches of oil over medium heat until it reaches 325°F; moderate the heat to maintain this temperature as you cook.

Armed with two metal tablespoons, scoop up some kakiage mixture with one spoon and use the other to slowly slide the mixture into the oil. The first bits of batter to hit the oil will puff up and serve as a life preserver for the rest, keeping them afloat until the oil can work its crisping magic. Repeat until you have 4 or 5 floating vegetable webs, with about an inch of space around them. Bob and baste the fritters, turning once, until they are golden and crunchy all over, 2 to 2½ minutes.

5 Lift the fritters from the oil using a spider and lay them on the prepared baking sheet. Sprinkle with a tiny pinch of salt and repeat forming and frying fritters until all the mixture is used up. If the fritters become cold before they are all fried, reheat them briefly in a 350°F oven (do not hold them in the oven or they will become soggy).

6 Serve the hot kakiage with soy dipping sauce.

SOY DIPPING SAUCE
MAKES ABOUT 1 CUP

Bonito flakes add smoky depth to this sauce. Find them at Japanese grocery stores and at many well-stocked supermarkets.

½ cup soy sauce

½ cup mirin

¼ cup sake or dry sherry

¼ cup bonito flakes

In a saucepan set over medium heat, combine the soy sauce, mirin, ½ cup water, sake, and bonito flakes. Bring to a full rolling boil; then remove the pan from the heat and let cool. Strain the cooled sauce, discarding the solids. The sauce will keep in an airtight container in the fridge forever.

SOUPS AND STEWS

THAI-STYLE
NOODLE CURRY

SERVES 4

1 (15-ounce) can coconut milk

1 tablespoon coriander seeds

1 teaspoon cumin seeds

½ teaspoon yellow mustard seeds

3 fresh or dried small hot red chiles, such as bird's-eye chiles or chiles de árbol

¾ cup chopped shallots (about 3), plus thinly sliced raw shallots for garnish

¼ cup garlic cloves

1 bunch of cilantro, with roots if possible, leaves picked and stems and roots chopped, separated

1 (3-inch) piece of fresh ginger, peeled and sliced into coins

1 (1-inch) piece of fresh turmeric, peeled and sliced into coins, or 1 tablespoon ground turmeric

ingredients continue

My favorite Thai noodle soup, *khao soi,* is a melding of fresh curry paste simmered with rich coconut milk and garnished with chile oil. The result is addictively delicious, though I find it too heavy to eat a whole bowl. In this version, sweet potato is simmered along with the broth, then pureed. The result is still thick and comforting, with about half the fat.

1 Put the unopened can of coconut milk in the freezer for 15 minutes to solidify the layer of cream at the top.

2 In a small dry skillet set over medium heat, toast the coriander, cumin, and mustard seeds, shaking the pan frequently so they don't burn, until fragrant and a few mustard seeds pop and dance in the pan, about 1 minute. Pour them onto a plate and let cool. If using dried chiles, put them in the pan and toast, turning, until they puff, soften, and turn bright red, about 30 seconds. Set them on the plate with the spices to cool; if the chiles were cooked enough, they will become brittle as they cool. If they are still pliable, set them back in the pan for another 30 seconds. Pound the spices and dried chiles (if using) in a mortar until they are coarsely ground. Add the fresh chiles (if using), chopped shallots, garlic, cilantro stems, ginger, and turmeric to the mortar, and continue pounding until you create a paste, about 10 minutes. You can also do this in a food processor (crack the spices with the bottom of a skillet before adding).

recipe continues

1 large orange-fleshed sweet potato (about 1 pound), peeled and cut into 1-inch pieces

12 ounces shredded cooked chicken or cubed tofu

1 tablespoon fish sauce, plus more as needed

1 tablespoon light brown sugar, plus more as needed

1 tablespoon fresh lime juice, plus lime wedges for serving

1 teaspoon kosher salt

1 pound fresh Chinese-style egg noodles

Chile oil

3 Open the can of coconut milk and spoon the solid cream that has collected at the top of the can into a medium heavy pot. Set the pot over medium heat and melt the coconut cream. Add the curry paste and stir, frying it in the fat until the paste and fat become one smooth mixture, about 1 minute. Reduce the heat to low and continue stirring until the paste has darkened a shade and some orange oil begins to seep from the paste, about 8 minutes. Stir in the coconut milk, sweet potato, and 3 cups water. Increase the heat to medium-low and bring to a simmer. Cook, stirring often, until the sweet potatoes are very soft, about 30 minutes. Let cool slightly; then puree in a blender or with an immersion blender until smooth. Strain the curry through a fine-mesh sieve into a clean pot. Stir in the chicken, fish sauce, brown sugar, lime juice, and salt. Taste and adjust the seasoning with a splash of fish sauce or pinch of brown sugar, as desired.

4 Bring a large pot of water to a boil and add the egg noodles. Cook until tender, about 2 minutes. Drain and rinse the noodles under cool running water. Divide the noodles among 4 deep bowls. Ladle the curry over the noodles. Garnish with thinly sliced shallots, cilantro leaves, a squeeze of lime, and a drizzle of chile oil.

TIP: Curry paste tastes best when made with a mortar and pestle. You can get a good one for as little as $30 on Amazon, though any kitchen store will have options, too. Look for a 4-cup granite model, which is large enough to make batches of curry paste and pesto, and small enough to crush a few tablespoons of seeds or spices.

CHICKEN AND
DUMPLINGS

SERVES 4

4 bone-in, skin-on chicken thighs (about 1½ pounds)

Kosher salt

4 cups chicken broth

½ teaspoon black peppercorns

1 bay leaf

½ large onion

1 tablespoon all-purpose flour

Most regions in the United States claim some variation of chicken and dumplings. This simplified version uses chicken thighs and dumplings made of Sweet Potato Gnocchi dough (page 98). Lightly sweet and not too starchy, the dumplings add delicious contrast to a savory stew that is satisfying without feeling heavy.

1 Preheat the oven to 350°F. Line a rimmed baking sheet with parchment paper or foil.

2 Slide your fingers under the skin of the chicken thighs to loosen and peel off the skin in one piece. Flatten the chicken skins in a single layer on the prepared baking sheet. Sprinkle with a little salt and bake until they're crispy, about 20 minutes. Let the skins cool on a plate and reserve 1 tablespoon of the drippings.

3 Meanwhile, place the chicken thighs in a large, wide saucepan and cover with the chicken broth. Add 1 teaspoon salt, the peppercorns, bay leaf, and onion half. Bring to a simmer over medium heat and poach until the chicken is cooked through, about 25 minutes. Set the thighs on a plate and strain the broth, discarding the solids. Wipe out the saucepan.

4 Set the clean pan over medium heat and add the reserved chicken drippings. Whisk in the flour and let the mixture bubble, stirring, for 1 minute. Pour in the reserved strained broth and whisk until smooth. Cook the broth until it thickens, about 5 minutes. Meanwhile, shred the chicken into bite-size pieces, discarding any bones and fat.

1 medium carrot, cut into
½-inch coins

1 cup thinly sliced sugar snap
peas or shelled English peas

½ recipe Sweet Potato Gnocchi
(page 98), formed into ½-inch
dumplings

2 tablespoons chopped fresh
herbs, like chives, tarragon,
and/or thyme

Freshly ground black pepper

Pecorino or Parmesan cheese
(optional)

5 Add the carrots to the thickened broth and simmer until they are
halfway cooked, about 3 minutes. Stir in the peas and cook another
3 minutes. Fold in the chicken, reduce the heat to low, and keep the
stew warm while you cook the dumplings. If serving later, cool the
chicken stew; it can be refrigerated for up to 3 days or frozen for
1 month. Rewarm before proceeding.

6 Bring a large pot of water to a boil, salt it, and add the dumplings.
Poach the dumplings until they float and more than half of each
dumpling is bobbing above the surface of the water, about 3 minutes.
Remove them with a spider and add to the pot of chicken stew. Add
the herbs to the pot and give the chicken and dumplings a gentle stir
to incorporate the dumplings and herbs. Return to a simmer; then
remove from the heat and spoon into serving bowls. Top each serving
with a grind of pepper and use a vegetable peeler to shave off a few
ribbons of cheese, if desired. Crumble a chicken skin over each bowl
and serve.

TIP: You can cook this dish a day ahead, let it cool, and store it in the refrigerator overnight. When you're ready to eat, rewarm it gently on the stove.

BRAISED SAUSAGE,
LENTILS, AND WHITE SWEET POTATOES

SERVES 4

1 tablespoon olive oil

1 pound pork or chicken
Italian sausage (4 or 5 links),
preferably a mix of spicy
and sweet

1 large onion, sliced into
¼-inch-thick half-moons

6 garlic cloves

2 tablespoons tomato paste

Pinch of dried red chile flakes
(optional)

½ cup white wine

1 cup French green lentils,
picked over and rinsed

1 large Hannah or other white-
fleshed sweet potato (about
1 pound), peeled and cut into
1-inch wedges

2 tablespoons chopped fresh
rosemary

1 bay leaf

3 cups chicken broth

Kosher or fine sea salt

This soulful one-pot meal can be pulled together in less than an hour, but it eats like a braise that cooked all day. The sausages plump and become tender as they cook slowly along with the creamy sweet potatoes and lentils. Pair with a Pinot Gris, and you have a meal fit for company.

1 Preheat the oven to 325°F.

2 Heat the olive oil in a 5- to 6-quart Dutch oven over medium heat. Add the sausages and cook, turning with tongs to color evenly, until browned all over, 5 to 6 minutes. Remove the sausages to a plate and add the onion and garlic to the pot. Stir to coat in the fat and reduce the heat to medium-low. Cook the onion and garlic until they are limp and pick up a bit of color, about 8 minutes. Stir in the tomato paste and chile flakes, if using, working the paste into the onions and garlic until the oil in the pan is terra-cotta colored, 2 to 3 minutes. Pour the white wine into the pot and stir, scraping up any browned bits on the bottom of the pot. Simmer until the liquid is reduced by half, about 3 minutes.

3 Add the lentils, sweet potato, rosemary, and bay leaf. Snuggle the sausages into the pot. Pour the broth over everything and season lightly with salt. Increase the heat to medium and bring to a simmer. Cover and slide the pot into the oven. Braise until the sausages are tender, the lentils and sweet potatoes are cooked through, and most of the liquid is absorbed, about 40 minutes. Let rest for 15 minutes before serving.

MISO SOUP
WITH GINGER AND TOFU

Crunchy threads of ginger and umami-packed miso contrast with the earthy sweet potatoes in this soup. Fortified with tofu, this dish is super satisfying. Dashi is one of those recipes that seems intimidating, but it is the fastest fresh broth you can make. It has two ingredients: kombu, a variety of dried seaweed, and bonito flakes, which look like wood shavings and are made of dried tuna. Both can be stored in the pantry indefinitely and are carried in Japanese grocery stores and at many well-stocked supermarkets. Should you have some chicken or vegetable stock on hand, it will also work well.

SERVES 4

4 cups Dashi (recipe follows)

1 large orange- or white-fleshed sweet potato (about 1 pound), peeled and cut into ½-inch cubes

1 scallion, green and white separated and thinly sliced

1 (1-inch) piece of fresh ginger, peeled and julienned

8 ounces firm tofu, cut into ½-inch cubes

¼ cup white miso

Kosher or fine sea salt (optional)

1 Combine the dashi, sweet potato, scallion whites, and ginger in a large saucepan over medium-high heat. Bring to a simmer, then reduce the heat and cook gently until the sweet potatoes are tender, about 15 minutes. Stir in the tofu.

2 Place the miso in a small bowl and add about ¼ cup of the hot dashi from the pot. Use the back of a spoon to mash the miso into the broth, forming a slurry. Pour the slurry into the pot and stir gently to combine. The soup should be a little sweet and salty and full of umami. Season to taste with salt, if necessary; then remove the pot from the heat and ladle the soup into serving bowls. Garnish with the scallion greens.

DASHI
MAKES 4 CUPS

2 (3-inch) squares of kombu

4½ cups cool water

½ cup bonito flakes (optional)

TIP: Avoid using purple sweet potatoes in soups, since their pigment will bleed and turn the broth an unappetizing grayish-blue color.

Place the kombu in a medium saucepan and cover with the cool water. Let soak for 10 minutes. Set the pan over medium heat and bring nearly to a simmer, just until tiny bubbles collect on the bottom of the pot and all over the kombu, and steam rises from the water. Add the bonito flakes, if using, remove the pan from the heat, and steep for 20 minutes. Strain the dashi and discard the solids. Let the dashi cool to room temperature and refrigerate until ready to use. The dashi will keep in an airtight container in the refrigerator for 3 days.

SWEET POTATO, CELERIAC, AND
SCALLOP CHOWDER

I first made this recipe on a cold and rainy November day after a trip out to the northern tip of Long Island. I had visited a farmer who loaded me up with root vegetables and pointed me in the direction of an excellent fish market. It was the first week of bay-scallop season, so I grabbed a pint and headed home to warm up with this chowder. Since it uses root vegetables, like celeriac and sweet potatoes, it is much heartier than chowders that call for summer vegetables like celery, corn, and tomatoes.

SERVES 4 TO 6

4 tablespoons (½ stick) unsalted butter

4 thick-cut bacon slices, chopped

1 big leek, white part only, chopped

1 large orange- or white-fleshed sweet potato (about 1 pound), peeled and cut into ½-inch pieces

1 large knob celeriac (about 12 ounces), peeled and cut into ½-inch pieces

1 large waxy potato, such as Yukon Gold (about 8 ounces), peeled and cut into ½-inch pieces

2 bay leaves

1 Melt the butter in a large pot set over medium heat. Add the bacon and cook, stirring, until it is rendered and crisp, about 5 minutes. Remove the bacon with a slotted spoon and set on a paper-towel-lined plate to drain. Add the leek to the fat in the pan and cook, stirring occasionally, until translucent, about 5 minutes. Add the sweet potato, celeriac, potato, bay leaves, thyme, and clam juice. Bring to a simmer and taste the broth; the saltiness can vary depending on which cooking liquid you choose. Season with salt until it is pleasantly but not overwhelmingly salty, at least a teaspoon and likely more, as the vegetables will absorb a lot of salt as they cook. Reduce the heat to medium-low and gently simmer until the vegetables are tender, 20 to 30 minutes. (This is a good place to stop if you are making the chowder ahead of time.)

1 tablespoon chopped fresh thyme

4 cups clam juice, fish fumet, or chicken broth

Kosher salt

1 tablespoon cornstarch

1 tablespoon cold water

1 pint bay scallops

1 cup heavy cream

2 tablespoons chopped scallions (white and green parts) or chives

½ teaspoon freshly ground black pepper

Crusty bread, for serving

2 In a small bowl, stir the cornstarch and cold water until smooth. Drizzle the mixture into the simmering liquid and stir. The chowder should thicken just slightly. Stir the scallops into the chowder and return to a simmer. Cook for exactly 1 minute before removing the pan from the heat. Stir in the cream, scallions, and pepper. Serve piping hot with crusty bread for dunking. Pass the crispy bacon bits for sprinkling over the chowder.

TIP: This chowder is best made with whatever mild, fresh seafood you can find: clams, shrimp, and haddock would all be welcome instead of scallops.

SWEET POTATO LEAF AND
FAVA BEAN STEW

SERVES 4 TO 6

½ cup palm, coconut, or peanut oil

1 pound bone-in beef suitable for stewing, such as shank, ribs, or oxtail, cut into 1-inch-thick chunks (optional)

1 large onion, chopped

1 Scotch bonnet pepper

2 bouillon cubes, preferably Maggi

1 small salted and smoked dried fish (about 4 ounces)

2 large bunches of sweet potato leaves (about 2 pounds), washed

½ cup unsweetened, unsalted smooth peanut butter

1 cup cooked dried fava or butter beans or 1 cup fresh fava beans or edamame

Cooked long-grain rice, for serving

My cousin Emily is from the South and has traveled and worked extensively in West Africa. Her descriptions of eating the addictively spicy, peanut-spiked meat-and-vegetable dish called *plasas,* which is served over rice, led me to request this recipe from her and her husband, Nouhou, who grew up in Niger. Southern cooks, whose culinary traditions are forever intertwined with West Africa, may recognize the combination of beans and greens simmered with meat.

Sweet potato leaves are commonly found in the produce section of Asian grocery stores. And, if your grocery store has a machine that grinds peanuts into peanut butter, use that for this recipe. When shopping for smoked or salted dried fish, look for ones that are 4 to 6 inches long and are dry but pliable, like jerky. If you can't find fish like these, use a similar weight of bacalao (salt cod), soaked in water overnight, or a lean smoked whitefish. Omit the meat for a lighter stew.

1 Heat the oil in a large, heavy pot set over medium heat. Add the beef, if using, and onion and stir to coat them in the oil. Cook until the meat is opaque on the outside and the onion is translucent, about 8 minutes. Add the Scotch bonnet, bouillon cubes, and 4 cups of water. Cover and simmer until the meat is cooked through, about 30 minutes. Add the fish and continue simmering until the fish is tender, 15 to 20 minutes longer.

TIP: Feel free to use just a slice of Scotch bonnet, or substitute a less piquant chile pepper, if you are sensitive to heat.

2 Meanwhile, prepare the sweet potato leaves: Roll several leaves and their tender stems together like a cigar, and then thinly slice them crosswise into $1/8$-inch-thick ribbons. You should end up with 8 to 10 packed cups of sliced greens.

3 When the meat and fish are ready, remove them from the broth. Pull the meat from the bones and cut it into bite-size pieces; discard the bones. Flake the fish, discarding the skin and bones.

4 Return the broth to a boil over medium-high heat. Place the peanut butter in a small heatproof bowl and add $1/4$ cup of hot broth. Mash the peanut butter with the back of a spoon to incorporate the broth, adding more as needed until you have a smooth, pourable sauce. Add the peanut sauce to the pot and stir well.

5 Stir in the sweet potato leaves and beans, and simmer until they are warmed through and tender, about 10 minutes. Stir in the meat and fish. Simmer until a ring of oil forms around the edges of the pot and the stew has thickened, about 10 more minutes. Serve hot over rice.

SIDE DISHES

BABY SWEET POTATOES
A LA PLANCHA

Cooking *a la plancha* is a Spanish technique that entails quick cooking on a blazing hot sheet of steel so that the food retains moisture and tenderness. Popular with seafood, it works remarkably well with small root vegetables to create charred texture without overcooking the flesh. This is a super-simple recipe that requires you to pick through the farmer's market bin for the smallest sweet potatoes. Since they are only seared, it is important that they be small enough to cook through in a short time before they scorch.

SERVES 4

8 baby sweet potatoes (about 1 pound)

1 teaspoon neutral oil, such as canola or grapeseed

4 tablespoons (½ stick) cold unsalted butter, cut into 16 pieces

1 orange

1 teaspoon Maldon or other flaky sea salt

1 Scrub the sweet potatoes and cut them lengthwise into ½-inch thick planks. Rub their cut sides with the oil.

2 Preheat a large steel or cast-iron griddle over medium-high heat until very hot, about 5 minutes. Put the sweet potatoes on the griddle, cut-side down, and sear until they are darkly caramelized but not quite burned, about 4 minutes. Quickly flip them and dot each half with a piece of the butter. Let the butter melt and drip onto the pan, where it will brown. Zest the orange over the sweet potatoes. Cut the orange in half and squeeze one half over the sweet potatoes. Cook until the juice bubbles up and thickens like caramel, about 1 minute.

3 Transfer the sweet potatoes to a platter and drizzle with the sauce that has accumulated on the griddle. Sprinkle with the salt.

TIP: Cooking a la plancha can get smoky, so be sure to work in a well-ventilated kitchen or outdoors.

WHITE SWEET POTATOES WITH
CHIMICHURRI

Steak and sweet potatoes are similar in that they both are perfect foods on their own, completely delicious when lightly seasoned and simply cooked. They are also equally improved with the addition of classic Argentine chimichurri. The real stuff is made from bracing red wine vinegar, dried and fresh herbs, garlic, and lots of good olive oil—and it's even better if you give it several hours to sit and let the flavors meld.

SERVES 4

CHIMICHURRI

4 garlic cloves

1 tablespoon dried oregano

1 teaspoon dried red chile flakes

1 teaspoon kosher salt

¼ cup red wine vinegar

2 cups fresh parsley leaves

½ cup best-quality extra-virgin olive oil

4 medium white-fleshed sweet potatoes (about 2 pounds)

1 **Make the chimichurri:** Finely chop the garlic and put it into a jar. Add the oregano, chile flakes, and salt, and then stir in the vinegar. Let stand for 20 minutes. Finely chop the parsley and stir it and the olive oil into the vinegar mixture. Let stand at room temperature for 1 hour, or cover and refrigerate for up to 2 days.

2 Oven-roast (see page 18) or coal-roast (see page 20) the sweet potatoes. When they are just cool enough to handle, crack them down the middle and press the skin to break up the flesh a bit. Arrange the sweet potatoes split-side up and generously dress each with several spoonfuls of chimichurri. Serve any remaining sauce alongside for additional slathering.

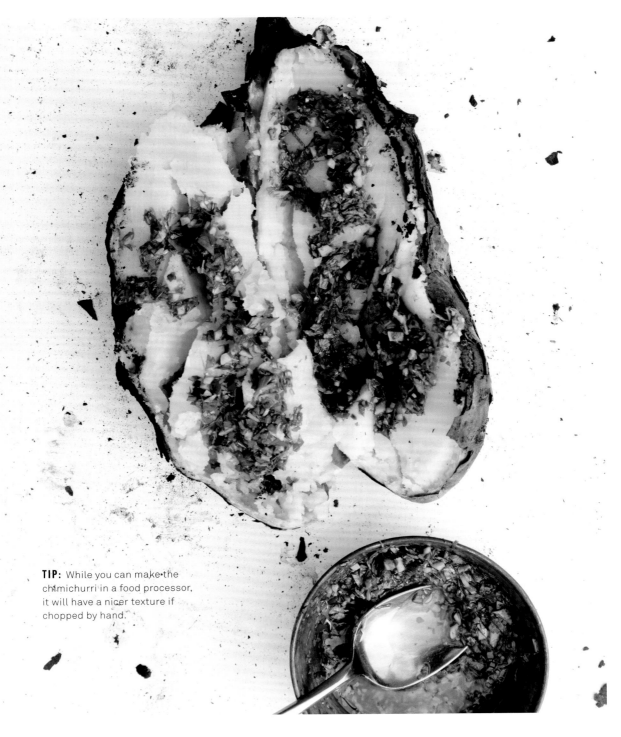

TIP: While you can make the chimichurri in a food processor, it will have a nicer texture if chopped by hand.

CRACKED SWEET POTATOES WITH CHILES AND COCONUT

SERVES 4

2 pounds Oven-Roasted (page 18) or Coal-Roasted (page 20) Sweet Potatoes (a few colors is nice), warm or at room temperature

2 tablespoons coconut oil or unsalted butter

1 tablespoon peeled and minced fresh ginger

1 serrano chile, sliced into rings

2 scallions, whites and greens separated and chopped

1 tablespoon fresh lime juice

1 teaspoon fish sauce

1 teaspoon honey (optional)

2 tablespoons unsweetened coconut flakes, toasted

2 tablespoons chopped fresh mint

I made this dish for the first time when I was "detoxing" between recipe-testing cookbooks. I had a few leftover roasted sweet potatoes and other odds and ends in the fridge, so I warmed them up and assembled them on a platter. The combination of colorful sweet potatoes, spicy chile, funky fish sauce (trust me on this one!), and fresh herbs is outstanding.

1 Crack open the sweet potatoes and spoon chunks of the flesh onto a platter; discard the skins.

2 Melt the coconut oil in a small skillet set over medium-low heat. Add the ginger, chile, and scallion whites. Cook until the chile is softened but not browned, about 30 seconds. Remove the pan from the heat and stir in the lime juice, fish sauce, and honey, if using. Spoon the sauce over the sweet potatoes, scatter with the scallion greens, coconut, and mint, and serve.

SWEET POTATO
RISOTTO

Risotto gets its creamy texture from two sources: stirring the rice while it cooks to loosen the starch on the outside of each grain, and finishing the cooked rice with a heavy dose of butter and Parmesan cheese. The result is rich and delicious. In this recipe, sweet potato puree flavors and lightens the risotto while keeping it saucy and reducing the amount of dairy traditionally used. To make it a main course, stir in roasted mushrooms or top with fried sage and crispy prosciutto.

SERVES 4

4 cups chicken or vegetable broth

½ teaspoon kosher salt

1 tablespoon olive oil

½ cup chopped onion

1 cup Arborio rice

¼ cup white wine or apple cider vinegar

1 cup Sweet Potato Puree (page 25)

2 tablespoons unsalted butter

¼ cup finely grated Parmesan cheese, plus more for garnish

Freshly ground black pepper

1 Warm the broth in a small saucepan set over low heat until steaming. Season it with the salt and have a ladle handy.

2 In a large saucepan or deep skillet set over medium heat, combine the olive oil and onion, and cook, stirring, until the onion begins to soften, about 4 minutes.

3 Set a timer for 17 minutes. Add the rice to the saucepan, start the timer, and toast the rice, stirring until the edges of the grains are translucent, about 2 minutes. Add the wine; let it bubble up and reduce until the bottom of the pan looks dry, about 2 minutes. Stir in about $1/2$ cup of the warm broth. Stir it as it simmers, adding more broth by the ladleful as it is absorbed. You will use at least 3 cups of broth and perhaps more, depending on how much evaporates. When the timer goes off, stir in the sweet potato puree.

4 Remove the pan from the heat and stir in the butter and Parmesan. Divide among bowls and sprinkle with Parmesan and black pepper.

GRILLED SWEET POTATOES WITH
GARLIC-MAPLE GLAZE

SERVES 4 TO 6

½ cup (1 stick) unsalted butter

4 shallots, thinly sliced

1 head of garlic, cloves peeled

¼ cup maple syrup

Kosher salt

2 tablespoons white wine vinegar

4 medium sweet potatoes, peeled if desired, cut into ¾-inch-thick rounds

TIP: Grilling the blanched, cooled sweet potatoes without a slick of oil may seem counterintuitive. If the surface of the sweet potato is dry when it hits the grill, it will become deliciously crispy and charred over the hot coals. If they stick, try oiling the grate and using a metal spatula to turn the pieces.

Travis Flood, the chef at Pappas Artisanal in La Verne, California, volunteered to cook for Chefs Cycle, a 300-mile fund-raising bike ride for No Kid Hungry. On top of feeding some of the most discerning palates in the industry, each morning after breakfast, Chef Flood jumped on his bike and rode one hundred miles with the rest of the chefs to the next stop. These sweet potatoes, blanched, cooled, then grilled and glazed with caramelized garlic and maple syrup, made an appearance at breakfast one day and were the perfect fuel for our ride.

1 Melt the butter in a medium saucepan set over medium heat. Add the shallots and garlic. Stir to ensure they are submerged, then reduce the heat to low. Cook, gently swirling the pot occasionally until the shallots and garlic are completely soft, 30 to 40 minutes. Remove the pan from the heat and stir in the maple syrup and 1 teaspoon of salt.

2 Bring a large pot of water to a boil. Add the vinegar and sweet potatoes, and cook until a knife inserted meets a touch of resistance, about 15 minutes. Do not overcook the sweet potatoes or they may fall apart when grilled. Drain them and arrange on a rimmed baking sheet in a single layer. Season with salt and cool completely.

3 Build a medium fire in a charcoal grill or heat a gas grill to medium. Grill the sweet potatoes around the edges of the fire, turning and rotating them to cook evenly until crispy and charred, about 3 minutes. Transfer to a bowl. Pour some glaze over the sweet potatoes and toss to coat. Season lightly with salt and serve the additional glaze on the side.

SAMBAL BUTTER

SERVES 4

SAMBAL BUTTER

2 Fresno or Holland chiles, stemmed and chopped

2 garlic cloves

½ teaspoon sea salt, plus more to taste

1 (1-inch) piece of fresh ginger, peeled and sliced

1 lemongrass stalk, trimmed and chopped

Grated zest and juice of 1 lime

½ cup (1 stick) unsalted butter, at room temperature

4 medium purple-fleshed sweet potatoes (about 2 pounds)

Neutral oil, such as canola or grapeseed

TIP: Roll the compound butter in parchment, wrap in plastic, and freeze for up to 1 month.

The ingredients mixed into compound butter release their flavor and aroma on contact with hot food, delivering a multisensory hit of freshness. Sambal—the fiery mix of chiles and garlic essential to Southeast Asian cuisine—turns the butter red and is a striking counterpart to the smoky, charred purple sweet potatoes.

1 **Make the sambal butter:** Pound the chiles and garlic with a mortar and pestle to coarsely mash. Stir in the salt and let stand for 10 minutes for the salt to dissolve and the flavors to blend. Add the ginger, lemongrass, and lime zest, and continue pounding until you have a smooth-ish paste, about 5 minutes. Squeeze in about a teaspoon of lime juice, and then stir in the butter with a fork until everything is well combined. Taste and add a bit more lime or salt, if desired. Roll the butter into a log and wrap in parchment paper, or pack it into a wide jar, and refrigerate until ready to use.

2 Oven-roast (see page 18) or coal-roast (see page 20) the sweet potatoes. Let cool slightly.

3 Heat a grill or broiler to medium-high.

4 Cut the sweet potatoes in half lengthwise and brush with a little oil. If grilling, lay the sweet potatoes, cut-side down, and grill until the flesh is charred, 2 to 4 minutes. If broiling, put the sweet potatoes on a rimmed baking sheet, cut-side up, and broil until the flesh is charred, 2 to 4 minutes. Top the cut sides with several pats of sambal butter.

TAMALES

Tamales are always described by their fillings—meat, beans, cheese, or vegetables—and not by the significance of the masa dough holding the filling. The base of the dough is corn that has been nixtamalized (soaked in an alkaline solution), ground to a paste, and whipped with lard and broth. The dough is spread on corn husks and stuffed with filling. One or two tamales deep and you start feeling stuffed yourself. This version uses mashed sweet potato in place of some of the lard and broth, which not only lightens the tamales but also adds a boost of vitamins and minerals.

MAKES 18 TAMALES

2 cups masa for tamales

9 cups hot water, plus more as needed

½ cup vegetable shortening or unsalted butter, at room temperature

1½ cups Sweet Potato Puree (page 25)

1½ teaspoons baking powder

1 teaspoon kosher salt

18 dried corn husks for tamales, soaked in warm water for 30 minutes

2 cups filling, such as refried beans, Sweet Potato Puree (page 25), or braised meat

8 ounces Jack or Cheddar cheese, cut into ½ × 2-inch batons

1 In the bowl of a stand mixer or in a large bowl, combine the masa and 1 cup of the hot water. Using the paddle attachment or your hands, mix until uniform, adding more water by tablespoonfuls until the masa is the texture of Play-Doh. Let stand for at least 10 minutes to thoroughly hydrate the masa. Turn the mixer to medium-low speed and add the shortening in three additions, alternating with the sweet potato puree in two additions. Stop the mixer, scrape down the bowl, and add the baking powder and salt. Continue mixing until the dough is smooth, about 1 minute. If mixing by hand, alternate beating the shortening and sweet potato puree with a wooden spoon or knead the dough by hand; add the baking powder and salt, and continue kneading until smooth.

2 Arrange the tamale dough, corn husks, and fillings on a work surface. Place a steamer basket in a large stockpot with a lid (a pasta insert is perfect). Use the back of a spoon or an offset spatula to spread a ¼-inch layer (about 3 tablespoons) of masa dough onto the wide half of a husk, spreading it to the edges. Repeat until you have 6 husks

spread with dough. Spoon 2 tablespoons of filling down the middle of the dough, top with a piece of cheese, then roll the tamale like a cigar. Fold the unfilled pointed end up along the seam of the roll. Stand the tamales, open end up, inside the steamer basket as they are filled. Repeat with the remaining ingredients until you have 18 tamales.

3 Soak a clean linen kitchen towel with water and drape it over the tamales, tucking its ends inside the pot. Set the pot over medium-high heat and add the remaining 8 cups hot water down the side of the pot. Cover the pot with the lid. Bring the water to a boil, then reduce the heat to medium to maintain steady steaming. Cook the tamales for 1 hour, replenishing the water in the pot as needed. Let cool slightly before serving.

TIPS: Tamales are easier to roll with large corn husks. Source them from well-stocked grocery stores or Mexican bodegas, or use banana leaves, found in the freezer section of many Asian grocery stores. Maseca is a brand of masa flour found in many American groceries and is used to make tortillas. This type of masa will work for tamales, but if possible, seek out a bag specifically labeled "masa for tamales," which contains a coarser grind of the flour and maintains a granular texture, even after long cooking.

PALAK ALOO

SERVES 4

Kosher salt

1 large sweet potato (about
1 pound), peeled and cut into
1-inch cubes

2 bunches of fresh spinach
(about 2 pounds) or
2 (10-ounce) packages frozen
spinach, thawed

3 garlic cloves

1 (1-inch) piece of fresh ginger,
peeled and sliced

1 serrano chile, stemmed

4 tablespoons (½ stick)
unsalted butter

1 teaspoon cumin seeds

1 medium onion, chopped

½ teaspoon garam masala

Cayenne pepper (optional)

¼ cup crème fraîche or heavy
cream

Naan, for serving

This is a take on the Indian restaurant staple of sautéed chunks of spiced potatoes served with a coarse spinach puree. It's perfectly fine to use frozen spinach, or whatever fresh greens are knocking around your produce drawer (maybe you have some sweet potato leaves?!). Serve with naan for swiping up every drop of the sauce.

1 Bring a large pot of water to a boil and salt it. Add the sweet potato cubes and boil until just tender, about 10 minutes. Using a spider, transfer the sweet potatoes to a paper-towel-lined plate; return the water to a boil.

2 Add the spinach to the pot of water and blanch it until it is tender and bright green, about 3 minutes for fresh and 1 minute for frozen. Lift from the water to a blender or food processor, dragging some of the salted water with the greens. Add the garlic, ginger, and chile to the blender, and pulse until the mixture is finely chopped.

3 Melt 2 tablespoons of the butter in a large skillet set over medium heat and add the sweet potatoes (toss the paper towel, but keep the plate handy). Add the cumin seeds and cook, turning, until the cubes are lightly browned, 4 to 5 minutes. Return the potatoes to the plate. Add the remaining 2 tablespoons butter and the onion to the skillet. Cook, stirring, until the onion is translucent, about 5 minutes. Pour the pureed spinach mixture into the skillet, folding to incorporate the onions. Add the garam masala and season to taste with salt and cayenne, if desired. Simmer gently, stirring and scraping the bottom of the pan often, for 5 minutes. Stir in the crème fraîche, then fold the potatoes back into the mix. Cook until the potatoes are heated through, 1 to 2 minutes, and serve hot with naan.

MAIN COURSES

BLACK DATE CHICKEN

SERVES 4

1 tablespoon neutral oil, preferably peanut

1 small onion, thinly sliced

1 tablespoon peeled and chopped fresh ginger

1½ pounds boneless, skinless chicken thighs, cut into 1-inch pieces

2 tablespoons fermented black bean paste or red miso

1 tablespoon chile-garlic paste (optional)

4 black dates or prunes, halved

3 scallions (white and green parts), cut into 1-inch pieces

1 large sweet potato (about 1 pound), peeled and cut into ½-inch cubes

1 celery rib, cut on an angle into ½-inch pieces

2 cups chicken broth

Kosher salt (optional)

2 teaspoons cornstarch

Steamed rice, for serving

This is a Chinese dish that has a hint of spice to cut through the smoky-sweet combination of black dates and sweet potatoes. Black dates are jujubes that have been smoked and dried; you can find them at Chinese grocery stores. If you can't find black dates, use prunes or pitted dates. Fermented black bean paste is also available at Chinese grocery stores.

1 Heat the oil in a wide, deep skillet set over medium-high heat. Add the onion and cook, stirring, until it softens around the edges, about 5 minutes. Add the ginger and cook 1 more minute. Add the chicken and roll it around in the onion. Cook, stirring occasionally, until the chicken is opaque on the outside, 3 to 4 minutes. Add the black bean paste and chile-garlic paste, if using, and swirl them into the onions and chicken. Let the sauces sizzle and dry out for 15 seconds before adding the black dates, scallions, sweet potato, and celery. Add the broth and bring to a simmer. Give it a good stir, cover, and reduce the heat to medium-low. Gently simmer until the chicken is cooked through and the sweet potatoes are tender, about 20 minutes.

2 Uncover and taste the sauce; it should be sweet and smoky, rich with a hint of spice and umami. Season with a pinch of salt, if needed. Whisk the cornstarch with 1 tablespoon water, and then whisk it into the sauce to thicken. Serve hot with steamed rice.

TIP: While you're at the Chinese grocery, pick up some greens, like bok choy or gai lan. Steam them to make it a meal.

IRISH FISH PIE

A staple in Irish and Irish-American households, fish pie is usually topped with a puree of white potatoes. But swap white potatoes for sweet potatoes, and it turns out that the mild brininess of the fish is fantastic with the slightly sweet topping. Feel free to substitute salmon or a mild white-fleshed fish for the cod, and shucked clams for the scallops. I find that piping the sweet potato puree onto the casserole is the easiest way to seal in the filling, though carefully spreading it with some patience also works.

SERVES 4 TO 6

½ pound fresh cod

½ pound large shrimp

½ pound bay scallops

6 tablespoons (¾ stick) unsalted butter, at room temperature

1 small onion, finely chopped

2 cups whole milk

2 bay leaves

2 fresh thyme sprigs

Kosher or fine sea salt and freshly ground black pepper

2 tablespoons all-purpose flour

¼ cup chopped fresh chives

2 cups Sweet Potato Puree (page 25)

1 Preheat the oven to 375°F.

2 Cut the cod into 1-inch pieces. Peel and devein the shrimp. Pick over the scallops for bits of shell, and if there is a tough band of muscle adhered to one side of each scallop, remove it. Refrigerate the seafood until ready to use.

3 Melt 2 tablespoons of the butter in a medium saucepan set over medium heat. Add the onion and cook, stirring, until translucent and soft, about 5 minutes. Pour the milk into the pan and add the bay leaves and thyme sprigs. Bring to a gentle simmer, stirring often. Stir ½ teaspoon of salt into the milk.

4 Poach each type of seafood individually: Place the cod in the simmering milk and cook until the fish is nearly cooked through, 1 to 2 minutes. Lift the cod from the milk with a slotted spoon and place it in a 2- to 3-quart casserole dish. Add the scallops to the milk and poach

recipe continues

until opaque, about 30 seconds. Lift from the milk with a slotted spoon and add to the dish with the fish. Add the shrimp and poach until they just begin to curl, about 1 minute. Lift them from the milk with a slotted spoon and add them to the dish. Use your hands or a fork to flake the cod into bite-size pieces. Season the fish with $1/2$ teaspoon salt and $1/4$ teaspoon pepper.

5 In a small bowl, mash 2 tablespoons of the butter with the flour. Remove the bay leaves and thyme sprigs from the milk. Bring the milk to a simmer once again and whisk the butter mixture into the milk until no lumps remain. Reduce the heat to low and simmer, stirring, until the mixture thickens, about 5 minutes.

6 Pour the béchamel over the fish in the casserole dish. Add the chives and fold gently to combine everything. Taste the filling and adjust the seasoning with salt or black pepper, if needed.

7 Reheat the sweet potato puree in the microwave, stirring every 30 seconds, or in a pot, stirring constantly, until warm. Stir the remaining 2 tablespoons butter into the sweet potatoes until it melts and season lightly with salt. If desired, transfer the warm sweet potato puree to a piping bag fitted with a star tip. Pipe or spread the puree over the filling, sealing the edges.

8 Bake until the filling is bubbly and the topping is browned, about 20 minutes. Let stand for a few minutes before serving.

COBB SALAD

SERVES 2

1 large sweet potato (about
1 pound), peeled and cut into
½-inch cubes

2 garlic cloves, sliced

1 tablespoon olive oil

1 tablespoon pimentón (mild
or hot) or good-quality smoked
paprika

1 teaspoon kosher salt

½ teaspoon freshly ground
black pepper, plus more for
serving

3 large eggs

1 small head romaine lettuce,
torn or shredded

1 avocado, peeled, pitted, and
cut into ½-inch pieces

1 medium tomato, cut into
½-inch pieces, or 1 cup halved
cherry tomatoes

¼ cup crumbled blue, feta, or
goat cheese

Buttermilk Chive Dressing
(recipe follows)

Roasting sweet potatoes with loads of smoky *pimentón* (Spanish paprika), black pepper, and garlic gives them a savory bacon-like punch that's so good in this salad you won't miss the meat. Serving the salad with strips of toppings is beautiful, and as a true chopped salad, the Cobb showcases lots of ingredients with different tastes and textures, all cut to about the same size.

1 Preheat the oven to 350°F.

2 In a medium bowl, combine the sweet potato, garlic, olive oil, pimentón, salt, and pepper. Toss to coat the sweet potato with the seasonings.

3 Heat a large ovenproof skillet over medium-high heat. Scrape the sweet potato cubes and all their seasonings into the skillet. Shake and toss the sweet potato cubes in the skillet until they begin to sizzle, about 30 seconds, and then slide the skillet into the oven. Roast until browned and tender, about 15 minutes. Let cool to room temperature.

4 Meanwhile, place the eggs in a small saucepan and cover with cold water. Set the pan over high heat and bring to a boil. Remove the pan from the heat and let stand for 7 minutes. Drain; shake the pan to crack the eggshells and then ice and cold water to cover. Let stand for 10 minutes to fully cool the eggs. Drain and peel the eggs. Cut the eggs into 1/2-inch pieces.

5 On a large platter or plate, arrange a bed of lettuce. Arrange the sweet potato, avocado, tomato, eggs, and cheese in strips on top of the lettuce. Grind pepper over the salad and drizzle with the dressing.

BUTTERMILK CHIVE DRESSING

MAKES ¾ CUP

¼ cup sour cream

¼ cup mayonnaise

¼ cup buttermilk or whole milk

¼ cup chopped fresh chives

1 teaspoon white wine or apple cider vinegar

½ teaspoon freshly ground black pepper

½ teaspoon kosher salt

In a small bowl, whisk together the sour cream, mayonnaise, and buttermilk until smooth. Stir in the chives, vinegar, pepper, and salt. Let stand for 10 minutes. Refrigerate until ready to use. The dressing will keep refrigerated in an airtight container for 3 days.

HUEVOS ROTOS
CON CHORIZO

In Spain, *huevos rotos,* the ultimate hot, salty, greasy, delicious late-night meal, is required after a few too many hours at *botellón* (a sanctioned loitering and drinking event for young adults who can't get into bars—like tailgating without sports). Literally translated as "broken eggs," this dish consists of a couple of sunny-side-up eggs fried in chorizo drippings and laid atop a mound of fried potatoes, peppers, and sausage or *jamón.* I love this version that uses sweet potatoes in place of the classic white potatoes, as the sweet potatoes don't soak up loads of oil while frying. And the spicy chorizo and peppers play beautifully off the sweet potatoes.

SERVES 2

Olive oil

8 whole Padrón peppers
or 1 Italian frying pepper,
cut into ½-inch rings

1 large sweet potato
(about 1 pound), scrubbed,
quartered, and cut into ½-inch-
thick rounds or half-moons

Kosher salt

8 ounces Spanish-style chorizo,
cut into 1-inch chunks

2 large eggs

1 In a large, heavy pot set over medium heat, heat 2 inches of olive oil to 350°F. Line a plate with brown paper or paper towels. Fry the peppers in the oil until their skins blister and brown, about 1 minute. Using a spider, lift them from the oil and drain on the plate. Fry the sweet potato rounds in the oil until cooked through and crisp, about 8 minutes. Remove to the plate with the peppers and season the vegetables with salt. Evenly divide the sweet potato rounds and peppers between 2 shallow serving dishes.

2 In a large skillet, heat 1 tablespoon olive oil over medium heat. Add the chorizo and cook, stirring, until heated through and the casings are singed, about 4 minutes. Divide the sausages between the dishes of vegetables. Crack the eggs into the hot chorizo oil. Fry the eggs, basting with the oil, until the whites are set and the yolks are still runny, about 2 minutes. Top each dish with an egg and serve immediately.

SWEET POTATO RAVIOLI
WITH SARDELLA SAUCE

Chef Gerard Craft cooks in St. Louis, Missouri, where he is responsible for changing the local restaurant curve. Diners can thank him for keeping standards high and the restaurant scene thriving (especially because he has mentored many other chefs). When I asked him for a recipe for this book, it was no surprise that he went over the top. Parmesan gives the ravioli's sweet potato filling a savory backbone. The sardella sauce—a spicy, fishy Calabrian pomodoro, and the namesake of one of his restaurants—boldly contrasts with the ravioli.

SERVES 4 TO 6

RAVIOLI

1 pound Oven-Roasted Sweet Potatoes (page 18)

¼ cup freshly grated Parmesan cheese

2 tablespoons olive oil

Kosher salt and freshly ground black pepper

Fresh Semolina Pasta Dough (recipe follows)

Semolina flour, for dusting

1 Make the ravioli filling: Remove the skins from the sweet potatoes and discard; place the sweet potato flesh in a food processor. Add the Parmesan and olive oil, and process until silky smooth. Taste and season lightly with salt and pepper. There will be about 1½ cups of filling; transfer it to a piping or plastic zip-top bag.

2 Fill the ravioli: Roll the pasta dough as directed. Use a 1½-inch ravioli stamp, biscuit cutter, or inverted glass to make 32 light indentations at ¼-inch intervals on half of the pasta sheets to mark where the filling will be piped. Pipe about 1 tablespoon of filling onto the center of each indentation. Gently lay a fresh sheet of dough over the filling. Press the top sheet down and around the filling, making sure to remove as much air as possible. Cut the ravioli with the stamp or cutter. Dust a rimmed baking sheet with semolina and place the ravioli on the semolina. Dust

SARDELLA SAUCE

¼ cup olive oil

1 medium yellow onion, chopped

3 tablespoons finely chopped garlic

3 smoked sardines in oil, drained, skin and bones removed

1 teaspoon Calabrian chile powder or hot paprika

¼ cup dry white wine

1 (28-ounce) can whole peeled tomatoes, pureed

2 tablespoons fish sauce

Kosher salt

¼ cup whole-milk yogurt (not Greek)

2 teaspoons honey

¼ cup fresh basil leaves

with a bit more flour, making sure they are not touching one another, tent with plastic wrap, and refrigerate until ready to cook, up to 1 day.

3 **Make the sardella sauce:** Heat the olive oil in a large, heavy saucepan or medium Dutch oven over medium-low heat. Add the onion and cook, stirring, until it is translucent but hasn't picked up any color, about 10 minutes. Add the garlic, sardines, and chile powder. Cook, using a spoon to break up the sardines until they are nearly a paste, about 3 minutes. Add the wine and let it bubble up and reduce by half, about 1 minute. Add the pureed tomatoes; rinse the can with ½ cup water and add the tomatoey water to the pot. Give the mixture a good stir, bring to a simmer, and cook for 10 minutes. Add the fish sauce, reduce the heat to low, and simmer very gently, stirring often so the sauce doesn't scorch. Cook until the strong flavors of garlic, fish, and chile have melded and mellowed, and the sauce has thickened, about 1 hour. Use the sauce immediately or let cool. Cover and chill for up to 3 days; reheat before proceeding.

4 Bring a large pot of salted water to a boil. Spread ½ cup of the sardella sauce on a warmed platter. Working in 2 or 3 batches, cook the ravioli until they are al dente, about 3 minutes. Lift the cooked ravioli from the water with a spider and nestle them into the sauce on the platter. When all the ravioli are cooked and plated, top with the rest of the sauce. Drizzle with the yogurt and honey, and scatter the basil over the top. Serve immediately.

TIP: In a pinch, use thin, fresh sheets of store-bought egg pasta to form the ravioli.

FRESH SEMOLINA PASTA DOUGH

MAKES ⅔ POUND

Semolina flour, made from durum wheat, has a gritty texture that contrasts with the softer all-purpose flour in this dough. It yields a "cat's tongue" texture so that sauce clings to the pasta. Seek it out at Italian groceries and most well-stocked supermarkets.

5 tablespoons semolina flour

3 tablespoons warm water

5 large egg yolks

1 cup all-purpose flour, plus more for dusting

1 In a small bowl, stir together the semolina and warm water with a fork. Beat the egg yolks into the semolina mixture.

2 Place the all-purpose flour in a medium bowl and make a well in the center. Pour the semolina mixture into the well and, using the fork, gradually incorporate the flour into the semolina. When the mixture becomes stiff, set the fork aside and knead the flour into the dough with your hands until the sides of the bowl are clean, about 2 minutes.

3 Dust a work surface lightly with all-purpose flour and knead the dough until it is smooth and glossy, about 8 minutes. Pat the dough into a disk, wrap in plastic, and let rest at room temperature for 30 minutes or in the refrigerator for up to 1 day.

4 Cut the dough in half. Wrap one half in plastic and set it aside. Flatten the remaining dough until it is thin enough to pass through a pasta roller's thickest setting. Pass the dough through the thickest setting, folding it in half between turns, until the dough is rectangular and uniform. Pass the dough through the thickest setting once more, this time without folding it. Adjust the roller to the next thinnest setting and pass the pasta sheet through it twice. Repeat this process until you get to the fifth setting; if the dough becomes sticky, dust with a little all-purpose flour. If the dough becomes too long to manage, cut it in half crosswise and continue rolling the pieces separately. Repeat this process with the wrapped dough half. Cover the pasta sheets with plastic wrap and refrigerate until ready to use, up to 30 minutes.

STIR-FRIED SWEET POTATOES
AND PORK

SERVES 2 TO 4

1 tablespoon Shaoxing wine or dry sherry

1 tablespoon soy sauce

1 teaspoon Chinkiang vinegar or Worcestershire sauce

½ teaspoon sugar

¼ pound ground pork

1 tablespoon neutral oil, such as canola or grapeseed

1 tablespoon chopped garlic

1 tablespoon peeled and chopped fresh ginger

3 scallions, whites and greens separated and chopped

Pinch of dried red chile flakes

1 large sweet potato (about 1 pound), peeled and grated in a food processor, julienned by hand, or spiralized (about 4 cups)

Freshly ground white pepper (optional)

The key to successfully making this dish is starting with sharply cut pieces of sweet potato. Grating the sweet potato on a box grater will make for ragged, wet pieces; take the time to either julienne the sweet potato by hand, grate it in a food processor, or spiralize it just before cooking. Stir-frying over high heat yields loose, crisp-tender pieces of sweet potato and pork.

1 Measure out all of the ingredients and assemble them near the stove. In a small bowl, stir the Shaoxing, soy sauce, vinegar, and sugar together. Place the pork in a medium bowl and pour the sauce over it; mix with a fork to combine.

2 Heat a wok or large, well-seasoned cast-iron skillet over high heat. Drizzle the oil around the inner perimeter of the pan, allowing the oil to glide down and coat the interior. Working quickly, add the garlic, ginger, and scallion whites, and stir with a wok spatula or wooden spoon for 5 seconds. Add the pork and chile flakes and stir, breaking it up with the spatula, until the pork is cooked through, about 4 minutes. Add the sweet potato and stir-fry, tossing and flipping until the pieces are half cooked, 3 to 5 minutes (or 5 to 8 if cooking in a skillet). Remove the pan from the heat. Season with a little white pepper, if desired, and garnish with the scallion greens.

CACIO E PEPE

This recipe is inspired by the classic Italian *cacio e pepe* (literally, "cheese and pepper") spaghetti. After a quick spin through a spiralizer, a sweet potato is transformed into noodles that are then quickly blanched before getting folded with a creamy black-pepper sauce. Cream, which is not traditionally used in cacio e pepe, helps bind the low-starch sweet potato noodles with the flavorful cheese and pepper for a super-delicious mac 'n' cheese wannabe.

SERVES 2

Kosher salt

1 cup heavy cream

1 teaspoon freshly ground black pepper

½ cup finely grated Pecorino Romano cheese

½ cup finely grated Parmesan cheese

2 large sweet potatoes (about 2 pounds), peeled and spiralized through the smallest (spaghetti-size) attachment

1 Bring a large pot of water to a boil and salt it.

2 Meanwhile, pour the cream into a large skillet set over medium heat and stir in the pepper. Bring to a simmer and reduce the cream by half, about 5 minutes. Remove from the heat and whisk in the cheeses until smooth. Keep the sauce warm.

3 Cook the sweet potato noodles in the boiling salted water until they are nearly tender, about 4 minutes. Reserve ½ cup of the cooking liquid and then drain the noodles. Add the noodles to the sauce in the skillet and fold to coat the noodles. Add splashes of the reserved cooking water as necessary to create a loose, creamy sauce that clings to the noodles. Divide among bowls and serve.

TIPS: This dish comes together in a snap; have all the ingredients ready to go before you start cooking.

PEPIÁN DE POLLO

This is a recipe from Antigua, Guatemala, which, because of the chiles and seeds that flavor and thicken it, is similar to a mole, but it's more of a rustic soup than a sauce for meat. I love making this dish in late summer and early fall, when beans and squash are in full supply and even getting a little tough, which means they'll benefit from long cooking.

SERVES 6

2 onions

3 pounds bone-in, skin-on chicken legs (about 4)

1 small bunch of fresh cilantro, leaves separated and stems reserved

Kosher salt

2 dried guajillo chiles, stemmed, seeded, and torn into postage-stamp-size pieces

¼ cup pepitas

3 tablespoons white sesame seeds

1 (4-inch) piece of baguette, torn into pieces

½ teaspoon black peppercorns

3 large garlic cloves, unpeeled

2 poblano peppers

1 Cut one of the onions in half and place it in a large, heavy pot with the chicken legs and the cilantro stems. Add 1 tablespoon salt and 8 cups water, or a bit more if needed to cover. Set the pot over medium heat. Bring to a simmer and then reduce the heat as needed to maintain a gentle bubble. Simmer until the chicken is just cooked through, about 20 minutes. Remove and discard the onion and cilantro stems, and the chicken skin, if desired. Let the chicken sit in its braising liquid in the pot on the back of the stove while preparing the sauce.

2 Meanwhile, in a large cast-iron skillet set over medium-low heat, toast the following ingredients in succession and put them on a plate as they deepen in color and aroma: the guajillo chiles, the pepitas, the sesame seeds, the baguette, and the peppercorns. Let everything cool. Place the toasted ingredients in a blender and add just enough of the chicken braising liquid to cover everything. Before blending, let this mixture soak for a few minutes while roasting the vegetables.

3 Cut the remaining onion into ½-inch slices. Wipe out any crumbs from the cast-iron skillet and set it over medium heat. Add the onion slices and roast in the dry skillet, turning once, until charred on both sides, about 8 minutes. Toss the onions into the blender. Add the garlic

1 pound plum (Roma) tomatoes
(3 to 4 medium tomatoes)

¼ pound tomatillos
(2 to 3 medium tomatillos)

1 pound sweet potatoes, peeled
and cut into 1-inch pieces

1 chayote or medium zucchini,
cut into 1-inch pieces

½ pound green beans

Steamed rice, for serving

Corn tortillas, for serving

cloves and poblanos to the skillet. Roast them, turning often, until they are charred all over, about 8 minutes. Put them on a plate to cool a bit, then peel away their skins and remove the stems and seeds; discard the skins, stems, and seeds. Add the garlic and poblanos to the blender. Finally, add the tomatoes and tomatillos to the skillet and roast until they become charred and their flesh begins to melt and collapse inside the skin, 10 to 15 minutes. Remove their cores and plop them into the blender. Add the cilantro leaves to the blender.

4 Process the contents of the blender until very smooth, at least 2 full minutes. (You just spent a half hour toasting everything perfectly; take the time to make it smooth!)

5 Return the pot with the chicken to medium heat and add the sweet potatoes, chayote, and green beans. Simmer until the vegetables are very tender, about 15 minutes. Stir in the chile-seed paste and season with salt to taste. Serve hot in shallow bowls with rice and corn tortillas on the side.

"BIG MACS"

As a kid, I loved the classic Big Mac, and I still occasionally get a taste-memory craving for it. But, as an adult, I really don't like the low-quality meat that's part of the original package, so I re-created the sandwich at home, replacing the meat with crispy sweet potato patties which go remarkably well with the tangy sauce, crunchy pickles, onions, iceberg lettuce, and American cheese, all on a sesame seed bun.

MAKES 4 BURGERS

2 large sweet potatoes
(about 1½ pounds), peeled

1 teaspoon kosher salt

½ teaspoon freshly ground
black pepper

Neutral oil, such as canola or
grapeseed

4 sesame seed burger buns,
plus 4 additional bottom buns

Burger Sauce (recipe follows)

¼ head iceberg lettuce,
shredded

24 dill pickle chips

4 slices American cheese

¼ cup thinly sliced onion or
shallot

1 Grate the sweet potatoes on a box grater into a large bowl. Season with the salt and pepper.

2 Heat the oil to a depth of ¼ inch in a large, nonstick skillet set over medium heat. Line a plate with brown paper or paper towels. When the oil shimmers, add 2 or 3 handfuls (about ½ cup each) of sweet potato to the skillet in compact mounds. Let the sweet potatoes fry into a patty, like a hash brown or latke, for about 2 minutes. Flip and cook until the patties are crispy, 2 more minutes. Drain the patties on the brown paper. Replenish the oil as needed to maintain a depth of ¼ inch. Repeat with the remaining sweet potatoes until you have 8 patties.

3 Toast the buns. Line up the 8 bottom buns on a work surface. Spread 1 tablespoon of burger sauce on each and then top with shredded lettuce and pickle chips. Place a slice of cheese on half (4) of the bottom buns and a patty on all of them. Top the patties with the onions, stack the burgers, and add the top buns.

BURGER SAUCE
MAKES ½ CUP (ENOUGH FOR 4 BURGERS)

TIP: The patties can be made up to 1 hour ahead; reheat them in a 400°F oven until hot and crispy, about 5 minutes.

¼ cup mayonnaise

2 tablespoons grainy mustard

1 teaspoon pickle juice

½ teaspoon honey

2 tablespoons chopped dill pickles

1 garlic clove, chopped

½ teaspoon paprika

In a medium bowl, whisk together the mayonnaise, mustard, pickle juice, honey, pickles, garlic, and paprika until smooth. The sauce will keep in an airtight container in the refrigerator for 3 days.

SWEET POTATO
GNOCCHI

SERVES 6;
Makes about 72 gnocchi

2 large white-fleshed sweet potatoes (about 1½ pounds)

1 large egg

½ ounce finely grated pecorino cheese (about ¼ cup)

1 teaspoon kosher salt, plus more as needed

¼ teaspoon freshly ground black pepper

Whisper of freshly grated nutmeg

1½ cups all-purpose flour, plus more for dusting

Gnocchi is one of those recipes that come with warnings: don't add too much flour or they will be tough; don't overwork the dough or they will be dense; don't overcook the dumplings or they will be slimy. Solution? Using white sweet potatoes in place of starchy russet potatoes means the dough is more forgiving if overworked, the dumplings won't overcook as easily, and the result feels lighter in your happy belly. This recipe makes loads of the fresh dumplings, so you can cook half tonight and freeze the rest for another time.

Since white sweet potatoes are available year-round, make these gnocchi often and try each of the accompanying seasonal sauces (see Sauces for Every Season, page 100).

1 Preheat the oven to 350°F. Line a rimmed baking sheet with parchment paper or foil.

2 Scrub the sweet potatoes, prick them in a few spots with a fork, and set them on the prepared baking sheet. Bake until the sweet potatoes are completely tender throughout, about 1 hour. Let cool.

3 When the sweet potatoes are cool enough to handle, split them open and scoop out the flesh. Press the flesh through a potato ricer or food mill into a large bowl, or finely mash it with a fork. You should end up with about 2 cups of mashed sweet potatoes.

4 To the sweet potato, add the egg, pecorino, salt, pepper, and nutmeg, and mix well with a fork. Add the 1½ cups flour and use the fork to

work it in, setting aside the fork once the flour is just incorporated. Use your hands to fold and press the dough into a ball. Put the ball on a lightly floured work surface and knead the dough just until it is uniform and slightly springy, about ten times.

5 Dust a rimmed baking sheet with flour. Divide the dough into 4 equal-size pieces. Dust the work surface with some fresh flour, and roll each piece of dough into a rope with a $1/2$-inch diameter. Cut the ropes at $1/2$-inch intervals with a knife or bench scraper (you can make them bigger or smaller to suit your taste; adjust cooking time accordingly). Dust them with a bit more flour, so they aren't sticky to the touch.

6 If you like, working with one at a time, use your thumb to roll each dumpling over the tines of a fork or a gnocchi paddle and onto the floured baking sheet. (The grooves and dimples that form on the surface of the gnocchi will help catch the sauce that dresses them.) Refrigerate until ready to cook. (Alternatively, freeze them on the baking sheet, making sure the gnocchi are not touching, until firm. Pop them off of the baking sheet and store in a plastic zip-top bag in the freezer for up to 1 month.)

7 Prepare one of the sauces that follow, if desired. Bring a large pot of water to a boil and salt it. Add two handfuls of gnocchi at a time, cooking them until they float and more than half of each gnocchi is bobbing above the surface of the water, about 3 minutes for fresh gnocchi and 4 to 5 minutes for frozen. Using a spider, transfer them to a waiting skillet or bowl and repeat with remaining gnocchi. (Remember to reserve cooking water, as needed, for finishing your sauce.)

SPRING
ASPARAGUS AND MINT

MAKES 3 CUPS

1 tablespoon olive oil

1 medium spring onion
or 4 scallions (white and green
parts), trimmed of roots and
tough tops, sliced

1 pound asparagus, trimmed
and sliced into ¼-inch coins

½ cup water reserved from
cooking the gnocchi

2 tablespoons unsalted butter

¼ cup finely grated pecorino
cheese

¼ cup thinly sliced fresh mint

Freshly ground black pepper

Fresh lemon juice

1   Heat the olive oil in a large
skillet set over medium heat. Add
the onion and asparagus, and cook,
stirring, until the asparagus is
bright green, 1 to 2 minutes.

2   Add the cooked gnocchi and
the ½ cup reserved cooking water.
Bring to a simmer and cook until
the sauce has thickened, about
1 minute. Stir in the butter; then
remove the pan from the heat and
stir in the cheese and mint. Season
with pepper and lemon juice to
taste.

SUMMER
NO-COOK BASIL POMODORO

MAKES 2 CUPS

1 pound very ripe beefsteak or
heirloom tomatoes

2 lemon zest strips

2 large fresh basil sprigs

¾ teaspoon kosher salt

¼ cup extra-virgin olive oil

Pinch of dried red chile flakes
(optional)

1   Cut the tomatoes into 1-inch
pieces. Place them in a large
bowl and add the lemon zest,
1 basil sprig, and the salt. Toss to
combine, making sure the basil
is submerged. Let stand at room
temperature while forming the
gnocchi, at least 1 hour.

2   Pass the tomato mixture
through a food mill or coarse sieve
to remove the skins and seeds. Stir
in the olive oil and chile flakes, if
using. Pick the basil leaves from
the remaining sprig and thinly
slice them.

3   Toss the hot gnocchi with the
sauce and sliced basil.

AUTUMN
CRISPY SAGE AND BROWN BUTTER

MAKES ½ CUP

½ cup (1 stick) unsalted butter

12 fresh sage leaves

Kosher salt and freshly ground black pepper

¼ cup finely grated Parmesan cheese

1   Melt the butter in a large skillet set over medium-low heat and add the sage. Fry until the sage is crispy, about 30 seconds. Remove the pan from the heat. Transfer the sage to a paper-towel-lined plate with a slotted spoon.

2   While the gnocchi cook, return the pan with the butter to the heat. Add the gnocchi and a splash of their cooking water, and bring to a simmer, shaking the pan to form a creamy sauce.

3   Season with salt and pepper. Divide among bowls and sprinkle with the crispy sage and Parmesan cheese.

WINTER
BLUE CHEESE WITH PRUNES

MAKES 1½ CUPS

1 cup heavy cream

3 fresh thyme sprigs

8 prunes, each cut into 4 pieces

½ cup crumbled Gorgonzola

Freshly ground black pepper

1   In a large skillet set over medium heat, simmer the cream with the thyme until reduced by half, about 10 minutes.

2   Remove the thyme and fold in the hot cooked gnocchi, prunes, and Gorgonzola. Stir to form a creamy sauce. Spoon into bowls and top with pepper.

TACOS

These are the perfect things to cook in the cooler months when you're craving all the smoke and spice that comes with outdoor cooking. The guajillo chiles in the salsa are mildly spicy, a delicious match for sweet potatoes. It's worth the extra effort to make the salsa for these tacos, but in a pinch, reach for the best-quality store-bought brand you can find.

SERVES 4; MAKES 12 TACOS

1½ pounds medium sweet potatoes, peeled and sliced into ½-inch rounds

1 teaspoon kosher salt

1½ teaspoons ground cumin

½ teaspoon ground coriander

1 tablespoon olive oil

12 small corn tortillas

Guajillo Salsa (recipe follows)

1 large avocado, peeled, pitted, and sliced

½ cup crumbled Cotija cheese

½ cup Mexican crema or sour cream

¼ cup thinly sliced scallions (white and green parts)

1 Preheat the oven to 375°F. Line a rimmed baking sheet with parchment paper.

2 Place the sweet potatoes in a large bowl. Season them with the salt, cumin, and coriander, and drizzle with the olive oil. Toss to coat the sweet potatoes and then arrange them in a single layer on the prepared baking sheet. Roast until tender and crusty brown, flipping once, about 20 minutes total.

3 Warm a tortilla in a large dry skillet set over low heat, flipping it once, about 20 seconds. Spread the tortilla with a little of the guajillo salsa and top with 2 or 3 slices of sweet potato, some avocado, Cotija, crema, and scallions. Repeat with the remaining tortillas and fillings, and serve.

GUAJILLO SALSA
MAKES 1 CUP

4 dried guajillo chiles

2 cups hot water

1 (1-inch thick) yellow onion slice

1 head of garlic, cloves separated but not peeled

¼ cup apple cider vinegar

2 teaspoons light brown sugar

1½ teaspoons kosher salt

1 Toast the guajillo chiles in a hot dry skillet set over medium heat, turning often, until they soften and puff, about 1 minute. Remove their stems and place the chiles in a bowl with the hot water. Place the onion and the garlic in the dry skillet and roast, turning often, until they are charred and softened, about 8 minutes. Peel the roasted garlic cloves.

2 Drain the chiles, reserving the soaking liquid (taste it, but don't use it if it is bitter—use fresh water instead). Put the chiles into a blender and add the onion, garlic, vinegar, brown sugar, and salt. Process until smooth, adding splashes of the reserved soaking liquid to loosen, if necessary. Cover and chill until ready to use. The salsa will stay fresh in the fridge for up to 1 week.

BREADS AND BAKED GOODS

SWEET POTATO
BISCUITS

There's a very simple trick to better biscuits: let them rest before baking. This provides time for the flour to hydrate and the gluten to relax, which yields a tender biscuit free of the flavor of raw flour. It's also key to have all of your ingredients very cold. I keep butter in the freezer, so when a craving strikes, I can grate 6 tablespoons and have a couple of pats left to slather on the hot biscuits.

MAKES 9 BISCUITS

2 cups all-purpose flour, plus more for dusting

1 tablespoon baking powder

1 teaspoon kosher salt

6 tablespoons (¾ stick) unsalted butter, frozen

1½ cups Sweet Potato Puree (page 25), chilled

Milk, for brushing

TIP: Make the dough ahead, shape the biscuits, and freeze them on parchment-lined baking sheets. When they are frozen, pop them into a plastic zip-top bag and keep in the freezer for up to 1 month.

1 Preheat the oven to 425°F. Line a rimmed baking sheet with parchment paper.

2 In a medium bowl, whisk together the flour, baking powder, and salt. Set a box grater into the bowl and grate the butter on the coarse holes directly into the flour mixture. Use a floured hand to knock off any flakes of butter from the grater. Add the sweet potato puree and stir with a wooden spoon until a sticky dough just comes together.

3 Dust a work surface with flour and turn the dough out onto it. Using floured hands, pat the dough into a rectangle. Fold the dough in half, pat it into a rectangle, give it a 90 degree turn, and then fold it in half again. Repeat this process for a total of five turns. Set the dough on the prepared baking sheet and use a rolling pin to roll the dough into an 8 × 8-inch square that is ½ inch thick. Refrigerate the dough on the baking sheet for 30 minutes.

4 Using a sharp knife and an up-and-down motion, cut the dough into 9 square biscuits. Scooch them ½ inch apart from one another and brush the tops with the milk. Bake until puffed and golden brown, 12 to 15 minutes. Serve warm.

SWEET POTATO
MILK BREAD DOUGH

This versatile dough is endlessly adaptable. Use it in the many variations in the following pages.

MAKES 3½ POUNDS DOUGH
Enough for two loaves, 32 rolls, or 24 hot dog buns

1 cup whole milk, warmed, plus more for brushing

5 tablespoons sugar

2¼ teaspoons active dry yeast (¼-ounce envelope)

1½ cups Sweet Potato Puree (page 25; start with 1 pound orange-fleshed sweet potatoes)

2 large eggs

4 tablespoons (½ stick) unsalted butter, melted, plus more for the bowl and the pans

1 tablespoon kosher salt

6 cups (27 ounces) all-purpose flour, plus more for dusting

TIP: You'll notice that the flour amounts are given in both volume and weight. Measuring either way is fine, but I find that, when baking, knowing the weight of flour is helpful, since it is a more accurate measurement.

1 In the bowl of a stand mixer or a large bowl, gently stir together the 1 cup warm milk, 1 tablespoon of the sugar, and the yeast. Let stand until the mixture becomes foamy, about 5 minutes.

2 Add the sweet potato puree, the remaining 4 tablespoons sugar, the eggs, butter, and salt to the yeast mixture. Fit the machine with the hook attachment and mix the ingredients on low speed until smooth, about 1 minute. With the machine running, add the flour, 1 cup at a time. When all of the flour has been added, increase the speed to medium and knead the dough until it is silky smooth, about 10 minutes. The dough should be smooth, soft, and a little sticky. (Alternatively, to make the dough by hand, whisk the sweet potato, the remaining 4 tablespoons sugar, the eggs, butter, and salt into the yeast mixture until smooth. Place the flour in a large bowl and make a well in the center. Pour the sweet potato mixture into the well and begin incorporating the flour with a wooden spoon. Continue stirring until the dough is too stiff to mix with the spoon. Lightly butter your hands and knead the dough in the bowl until it is smooth, about 10 minutes.)

3 Brush a large, clean bowl with some melted butter. Shape the dough into a ball and set it in the bowl, seam-side down. Cover the bowl loosely with plastic wrap and let rise in a warm spot until almost doubled in volume, about 1 hour. Punch the dough down and use immediately or refrigerate for up to 24 hours.

SANDWICH LOAVES

1 Prepare milk bread dough (facing page). Put a rack in the center of the oven and preheat it to 350°F. Always have the oven waiting for bread, not the opposite. Brush two 9 × 5-inch loaf pans with melted butter.

2 Turn the dough onto a lightly floured work surface and divide it into 2 equal pieces (each should weigh about 28 ounces). Working with one piece at a time, pat it into an oval that is about 10 inches long and ½ inch thick. Lift one short end and bring it to the center. Press it down with the heel of your palm. Turn the dough 180 degrees and fold the opposite side to the center of the dough, pressing again with your palm. Fold the dough in half in the same direction, using your palm to seal the dough. Transfer the shaped loaf to one of the pans, seam-side down. Press the dough down into the pan to spread it out evenly. Tent with plastic wrap; repeat with the remaining dough and loaf pan. (You can refrigerate or freeze the dough at this point, if baking later.) Let the dough rise until it is puffy and domes just over the top of the pan, about 30 minutes. (If frozen, defrost the bread dough for at least 24 hours in the refrigerator; let the chilled dough come to room temperature, about 2 hours, before baking.)

3 Brush the dough with milk and bake until golden and puffy, and the bottom of each loaf sounds hollow when tapped, 30 to 40 minutes. Let cool in the pans for 10 minutes before turning out and cooling completely on a rack, at least 1 hour. Slice with a serrated knife.

PULL-APART DINNER ROLLS

MAKES 32 ROLLS

1 Prepare milk bread dough from page 106. Arrange a rack in the center of the oven and preheat it to 350°F. Brush two 9-inch springform pans or one 13 × 9 × 2-inch baking dish with melted butter.

2 Turn the dough onto a lightly floured work surface and divide it into 32 equal-size pieces. The easiest way to do this is with a scale; each roll should weigh about 1½ ounces and be about the size of a small lime. Working with one piece at a time, pat it into a ½-inch-thick round. Gather the edges and press them into the center of the dough, forming a ball. Repeat with the remaining dough pieces. Line up the rolls, seam-sides down, in the pans. Tent with plastic wrap. (Refrigerate or freeze the dough at this point, if you're baking later.) Let the dough rise in the pans until puffy, 30 to 45 minutes. (If frozen, defrost the dough in the refrigerator, about 24 hours; let the chilled dough come to room temperature, 1 to 2 hours, before baking.)

3 Brush the dough with milk and bake until golden and puffy, about 25 minutes. Brush with melted butter, sprinkle with flaky salt, and let stand for 10 minutes. Remove the rolls from the pans and serve warm or at room temperature.

SPLIT-TOP HOT DOG BUNS

MAKES 24 BUNS

1 Arrange a rack in the center of the oven and heat it to 350°F. Brush one 18 × 13-inch rimmed baking sheet with melted butter (if it is made of aluminum, line the bottom with parchment paper and butter that, too).

2 Turn the dough onto a lightly floured work surface and divide it into 24 equal-size pieces, each about 2 ounces and the size of a tennis ball. Working with one piece at a time, pat the dough into a ½-inch-thick oval, and then fold it into thirds, like a letter. Fold it in half lengthwise, pinch to seal, and then roll gently into a 4-inch-long log. Repeat with the remaining dough. Line up the rolls on the prepared baking sheet and tent them with plastic wrap. (Refrigerate or freeze the dough at this point, if you're baking it later.) Let the dough rise on the baking sheet until puffy, about 30 minutes. (If frozen, defrost the bread dough for at least 24 hours in the refrigerator; let the chilled dough come to room temperature, about 1 hour, before baking.)

3 Brush the dough with milk and bake until golden and puffy, 20 to 25 minutes. Let cool and then carefully separate the rolls. Use a serrated knife to split the tops of the rolls lengthwise.

FLATBREAD

Some time ago, I worked at a restaurant near Parisi Bakery in the Nolita neighborhood of New York City. We ordered dinner rolls from this shop, and, being an old-school Italian bakery, the bakers used to gift us a loaf of their lard bread when they delivered our order. The classic bread—which is a great place to use the odds and ends of hard sausage or prosciutto—has a ribbon of chile-spiked lard swirling through the loaf. This flatbread is inspired by it and best eaten the day it is baked.

MAKES 1 FLATBREAD

¼ cup olive oil

½ recipe Sweet Potato Milk Bread Dough (page 106)

½ teaspoon kosher salt

½ teaspoon freshly ground black pepper

¼ teaspoon dried red chile flakes

2 ounces thinly sliced hard salami or pepperoni

2 ounces thinly sliced provolone cheese

2 tablespoons chopped fresh rosemary

1 Preheat the oven to 350°F. Coat a 13 × 9 × 2-inch baking dish with the olive oil.

2 Dump the dough into the baking dish and use your fingers to press the dough to fill the pan. Carefully pick up and flip the dough, coating both sides in the olive oil. Press your fingertips into the dough to make indentations in the surface and push it outward into the sides and corners of the baking dish. Once the entire dough is dimpled, cover the dough loosely with plastic wrap and set in a warm place to proof until puffy, about 30 minutes.

3 Remove the plastic and sprinkle with the salt, pepper, and chile flakes. Shingle the salami and provolone over the dough and sprinkle with the rosemary. Bake until the bread is golden and puffed, the cheese has melted, and the salami has given off some of its red oil, about 20 minutes. Remove the baking dish from the oven and let the bread cool for 10 minutes before slicing. Serve warm or at room temperature.

MAPLE PECAN
STICKY BUNS

MAKES 12 BUNS

SMEAR

½ cup (1 stick) unsalted butter

½ cup packed light brown sugar

¼ cup maple syrup

¼ teaspoon kosher salt

½ cup pecan halves

FILLING

¼ cup granulated sugar

¼ cup packed light brown sugar

⅛ teaspoon ground cinnamon

⅛ teaspoon kosher salt

½ cup chopped pecans

2 tablespoons (¼ stick) very soft unsalted butter

½ recipe Sweet Potato Milk Bread Dough (page 106), at room temperature

Neutral oil, such as canola or grapeseed, for the work surface

On an occasional Saturday morning when I was a kid, my dad would bring home sticky buns from a local bakery. The buns would arrive still warm, with lots of chewy caramel lacquering the edges. These sticky buns are inspired by those, but with less than half the sugar and fat of standard sticky buns. Sweet potato keeps the dough decadently moist and takes the place of much of the butter that would be found in brioche or any other rich dough that is traditionally used for sticky buns.

1 **Make the smear:** Combine the butter, brown sugar, maple syrup, and salt in a small saucepan. Set the pan over medium heat and cook until the mixture bubbles. Stir once and continue to cook until the mixture thickens and the bubbles pop more slowly, about 2 minutes. Pour the smear into a 13 × 9 × 2-inch pan, lifting the edges of the pan to distribute the smear and coat the bottom of the pan evenly. Sprinkle the smear with the pecans and let cool completely.

2 **Meanwhile, make the filling:** In a small bowl, combine the granulated sugar, brown sugar, cinnamon, and salt. Stir in the pecans.

3 Put the dough on a lightly oiled work surface and pat it into a rectangle with a long side near you. Using a rolling pin, roll the dough into a rectangle that is about 18 × 12 inches and ¼ inch thick; it is more important that the dough be ¼ inch thick than an exact-size rectangle.

4 Assemble the rolls: Using an offset spatula or the back of a spoon, spread the soft butter in a thin, even layer over the surface of the dough. Sprinkle the filling over the butter.

5 Beginning with the long side nearest you, lift up the edge of the dough and roll the dough away from you to form a tight coil. Pinch the edge of the dough to seal, and then place the roll on a parchment-lined rimmed baking sheet. Pop it into the freezer for 10 minutes.

6 Using a long serrated knife, cut the chilled log of dough into 1½-inch-thick rounds. Arrange the rounds, cut-side up, in the pan coated with the cooled smear, snuggling them together as needed. Cover the pan loosely with plastic wrap. Proof the dough at room temperature until puffy, 45 minutes to 1 hour. (Alternatively, let it proof slowly in the refrigerator overnight. Let the dough come to room temperature before baking, 1½ to 2 hours.)

7 Preheat the oven to 375°F.

8 Bake the buns until deeply browned and cooked through, 25 to 30 minutes. Remove the sticky buns from the oven and top them with a sheet of parchment. Invert a large platter or baking sheet over the sticky buns and flip them both at the same time, releasing the sticky buns onto the now parchment-lined platter. Scrape up any stuck caramel and pecans and drizzle over the buns. Let cool for at least 15 minutes before eating. Serve warm or at room temperature.

CHOCOLATE BABKA

A caramelized, crunchy, chewy, braided pull-apart bread, babka is a wonderful thing. Sweet potato keeps the dough moist and lends a striking orange color to the bread. Beautiful to look at, it's stunning at brunch or teatime, and it makes the best French toast of your life.

MAKES 2 LOAVES

½ cup (1 stick) unsalted butter, plus more for brushing

¼ cup plus 3 tablespoons sugar

¼ cup unsweetened cocoa powder

4 ounces good-quality milk chocolate, chopped

¼ teaspoon ground cinnamon

All-purpose flour, for dusting

½ recipe Sweet Potato Milk Bread Dough (page 106)

1 Melt the ½ cup of butter in a small saucepan set over medium heat. Stir in the ¼ cup of sugar and the cocoa until smooth. Remove the pan from the heat and add the chocolate and cinnamon. Stir until smooth and let cool, but do not refrigerate.

2 Line a rimmed baking sheet with parchment paper. Brush two 8 × 4-inch loaf pans with butter.

3 Lightly flour a work surface. Roll the dough into a rectangle that is about 16 × 12 inches and ½ inch thick. Using an offset spatula or the back of a spoon, spread the chocolate filling over the surface of the dough, leaving a 1-inch border all around. Starting with one long side of the dough, roll the dough tightly into a log, pinching the seam to seal. Carefully pick up the log and set it on the prepared baking sheet. Pop it into the freezer for 10 minutes.

4 Using a serrated knife, cut the dough in half lengthwise, exposing the layers of chocolate filling. With the cut-sides facing up, "braid" the two lengths of dough: take turns lifting one end of dough over

recipe continues

the other, always keeping the cut-side facing up. Pinch the ends to secure them and then cut the braided dough in half crosswise, creating 2 loaves. Lift each loaf into a prepared pan, snaking it like the letter *S*, if necessary, to fit. Tent the loaves with plastic wrap and let proof in a warm place for 30 minutes.

5 Preheat the oven to 350°F.

6 Remove the plastic wrap and bake the babkas until the loaves are golden and sound hollow when tapped, about 30 minutes.

7 Dissolve the remaining 3 tablespoons sugar in 3 tablespoons water. Brush the warm babkas with the sugar syrup. Run a knife around the edges of the babkas and let them cool in their pans. When cooled, turn out and slice them with a serrated knife.

ULTIMATE CREAM CHEESE
CINNAMON ROLLS

Make a batch of Sweet Potato Milk Bread Dough (page 106) on the Tuesday or Wednesday before Thanksgiving or any big celebratory weekend. Shape half of the dough into the Pull-Apart Dinner Rolls (page 108) for a dinner centerpiece, and use the other half to prep these cinnamon rolls to serve for breakfast the next morning. No hangover can resist the power of cream cheese frosting, I promise.

MAKES 9 ROLLS

4 tablespoons (½ stick) very soft unsalted butter, plus more for the pan

½ recipe Sweet Potato Milk Bread Dough (page 106), at room temperature

Neutral oil or butter, for the work surface

¾ cup packed light brown sugar

2 tablespoons ground cinnamon

ICING

6 tablespoons cream cheese, at room temperature

4 tablespoons (½ stick) unsalted butter, at room temperature

1½ cups confectioners' sugar

½ teaspoon vanilla extract

1 Butter a 9-inch square cake pan. Line a rimmed baking sheet with parchment paper.

2 Put the dough on a lightly oiled work surface and pat it into a rectangle with a long side near you. Using a rolling pin, roll the dough into a rectangle that is about 18 × 12 inches and ¼ inch thick; it is more important that the dough be ¼ inch thick than an exact-size rectangle.

3 In a small bowl, combine the brown sugar and cinnamon. Using an offset spatula or the back of a spoon, spread the soft butter in a thin, even layer over the surface of the dough. Sprinkle the brown sugar–cinnamon mixture over the butter.

4 Beginning with the long side nearest you, lift up the edge of the dough and roll it away from you into a tight coil. Pinch the edge to seal, and then place the roll on the prepared baking sheet. Pop it into the freezer for 10 minutes.

recipe continues

5 Using a long serrated knife, cut the chilled log of dough into 2-inch-thick rounds. Arrange the rounds, cut-side up, in the prepared cake pan, snuggling them together as needed. Cover the pan loosely with plastic wrap. Proof the dough at room temperature until puffy, 45 minutes to 1 hour. (Alternatively, let it proof slowly in the refrigerator overnight. Let the dough come to room temperature before baking.)

6 Preheat the oven to 350°F.

7 **Make the icing:** In a medium bowl, beat the cream cheese and butter together until smooth. Add the confectioners' sugar and vanilla, and beat again until smooth and fluffy, about 1 minute. Icing can be kept at room temperature for up to 1 hour; cover and chill for up to 3 days.

8 Bake the rolls until golden and cooked through, 20 to 25 minutes. Remove the pan from the oven and immediately spread the rolls with the icing. Let cool for at least 15 minutes before eating. Serve warm or at room temperature.

TIP: Make extra and freeze them: Shape the cinnamon rolls and arrange them 1 inch apart on a parchment-lined baking sheet. Freeze until frozen solid, then transfer to a gallon-size plastic zip-top bag. The day before baking, arrange them in a buttered 9-inch square cake pan, cover with plastic wrap, and defrost in the fridge. Let stand at room temperature until puffy, about 2 hours, before baking as instructed.

GINGERBREAD

MAKES ONE 9 × 5-INCH LOAF

¼ cup neutral oil, such as canola or grapeseed, plus more for the pan

1½ cups all-purpose flour, plus more for the pan

1 teaspoon ground cinnamon

½ teaspoon freshly ground black pepper

½ teaspoon baking soda

½ teaspoon kosher salt

¼ teaspoon ground cloves

1 cup Sweet Potato Puree (page 25)

2 large eggs

½ cup molasses

½ cup packed light brown sugar

¼ cup finely chopped, peeled fresh ginger or 1 tablespoon ground ginger

Gingerbread is evocative of cold-weather holidays, but I think it is one of the best anytime cakes to have around. The flavor of sweet potato is at home with fresh ginger and molasses, and the sweet potato keeps this cake moist for a couple of days after baking.

1 Preheat the oven to 350°F. Oil and flour a 9 × 5-inch loaf pan.

2 In a medium bowl, stir together the flour, cinnamon, pepper, baking soda, salt, and cloves. In a large bowl, combine the sweet potato puree, eggs, molasses, brown sugar, ginger, and oil; stir until smooth. Add the dry ingredients to the bowl with the wet and stir just to combine. Pour the batter into the prepared pan and tap the pan on the counter a few times to distribute the batter evenly.

3 Bake until the cake springs back when touched and a cake tester inserted in the center comes out clean, about 45 minutes. Let the cake cool for 20 minutes before transferring it to a rack. Let it cool completely before slicing.

SWEET POTATO
CAKE DOUGHNUTS

MAKES 18 DOUGHNUTS

Nonstick cooking spray

1¼ cups all-purpose flour

1 teaspoon baking powder

½ teaspoon ground cinnamon

¼ teaspoon kosher salt

2 large eggs

1 cup Sweet Potato Puree
(page 25)

¾ cup packed light brown sugar

½ cup vegetable oil

1 teaspoon vanilla extract

Confectioners' sugar (optional)

Orange glaze (see page 134, optional)

These crunchy cake doughnuts come together in a snap and are so delicious. Roast a couple of extra sweet potatoes the night before you want to make the doughnuts, and the dough will come together quicker than a bowl of cereal.

1 Preheat the oven to 350°F. Spray three 6-count doughnut pans with nonstick cooking spray.

2 In a medium bowl, whisk together the flour, baking powder, cinnamon, and salt. In a separate medium bowl, whisk together the eggs, sweet potato puree, brown sugar, oil, and vanilla until smooth. Whisk the wet ingredients into the dry until just incorporated. Transfer the batter to a piping bag or plastic zip-top bag, snip ½ inch from the pointed end or bottom corner of the bag, and pipe the batter into the pan.

3 Bake until golden, puffed, and a toothpick inserted into a doughnut comes out clean, 10 to 12 minutes. Transfer the doughnuts to a rack to cool. Dust with confectioners' sugar or drizzle with orange glaze. Serve warm.

SWEET POTATO
GALETTE

A delicious thing to eat at any time of day, this savory egg-topped galette is also quite pretty. Though simple to make, its wow factor is undeniable. Satisfying on its own at breakfast, all it needs is a tart salad to make the perfect lunch or supper. This recipe also works beautifully with other hard vegetables, such as delicata squash and Yukon Gold potatoes.

SERVES 2

All-purpose flour, for dusting

1 sheet (about ½ pound) frozen puff pastry, thawed

1 medium sweet potato (about ½ pound), peeled and sliced into ⅛-inch-thick rounds

¼ red onion or 1 shallot, thinly sliced

1 bacon strip, cut into ½-inch pieces

1 teaspoon fresh thyme leaves

Kosher salt and freshly ground black pepper

1 large egg

TIP: The galette may be assembled and stored in the refrigerator the night before you plan to bake it.

1 Preheat the oven to 375°F. Line a rimmed baking sheet with parchment paper.

2 Lightly dust a work surface with flour and unfold the puff pastry onto it. Using a rolling pin, roll the pastry into a 12-inch square. Place the puff pastry on the prepared baking sheet.

3 Shingle the sweet potato slices on top of the puff pastry, leaving a ½-inch border all around. Scatter the onion slices, bacon, and thyme over the sweet potatoes. Sprinkle the vegetables with a little salt and pepper.

4 Bake until the sweet potatoes are tender, the bacon is sizzling, and the pastry is puffed and golden, about 20 minutes.

5 Remove the baking sheet from the oven and crack the egg onto the galette. Sprinkle the egg with some salt and pepper. Return to the oven and bake until the egg white is set and the yolk is still a bit runny, about 6 minutes. Serve warm or at room temperature.

SWEET POTATO
WAFFLES

If you grew up on Bisquick, as I did, you might not realize that there's a difference between pancake and waffle batter. Though the ingredients are nearly identical, waffles are much richer, with quite a bit of melted butter or oil, countered with the lightening effect of whipped egg whites. Pressed in a hot iron, the finished texture is at once fluffy and crunchy, and one that holds up to a drenching of melted butter and syrup. Here, sweet potato takes the place of much of the fat and dairy.

SERVES 4

4 large egg whites

1½ cups Sweet Potato Puree (page 25)

1 cup buttermilk

4 tablespoons (½ stick) unsalted butter, melted

¼ cup sugar

1 tablespoon vanilla extract

2 cups all-purpose flour

2 teaspoons baking powder

½ teaspoon salt

Nonstick cooking spray

Maple syrup, soft butter, and/or cinnamon sugar, for serving

1 Preheat a waffle iron.

2 In a large bowl, beat the egg whites to soft peaks.

3 In a separate large bowl, whisk together the sweet potato puree, buttermilk, butter, sugar, and vanilla until smooth. Sift the flour, baking powder, and salt into the bowl and stir just to combine. Switch to a rubber spatula and fold the egg whites into the batter, a third at a time, until the batter is smooth with a few streaks of egg white still visible.

4 Spray the waffle iron with nonstick cooking spray. Add enough batter to just fill the iron, which will depend on its size. Close it and cook according to the manufacturer's instructions. Put the cooked waffle on a plate and serve immediately with syrup, butter, and cinnamon sugar, as desired. Repeat with the remaining batter. Leftover waffles may be cooled, wrapped, and frozen for up to 1 month. Toast as you would Eggos.

MUFFINS

Many a muffin was baked in the pursuit of this healthy, yet delicious recipe. Sweet potatoes provide a lot of moisture, a job done by refined oil in most muffin recipes; they also keep these muffins fresh for a couple of days. The tart, juicy raspberries shine against the wholesome batter.

MAKES 12 MUFFINS

Nonstick cooking spray

1½ cups peeled and grated sweet potato (from 1 medium)

1 cup all-purpose flour

¾ cup raspberries, fresh or frozen (unthawed)

1½ teaspoons baking powder

½ teaspoon salt

½ cup whole milk

¼ cup granulated sugar

2 tablespoons vegetable oil

1 large egg

½ teaspoon vanilla extract

¼ cup Demerara or turbinado sugar

1 Preheat the oven to 425°F. Spray 12 standard muffin cups or 24 mini muffin cups with nonstick cooking spray (be sure to spray the whole pan, including the area between cups). Line the cups with paper liners.

2 In a large bowl, combine the sweet potato, flour, raspberries, baking powder, and salt. Toss gently to combine, making sure the sweet potato and raspberries are well coated in flour. In a small bowl, whisk together the milk, granulated sugar, oil, egg, and vanilla until the sugar dissolves. Pour the liquid ingredients into the sweet potato mixture and stir with a wooden spoon until just combined. Scoop the batter into the muffin tins, filling each to the top of the paper liner. Sprinkle each muffin with about a teaspoon of Demerara sugar.

3 Bake until a cake tester inserted into the center of a muffin comes out clean, about 20 minutes. Let cool for 5 minutes before turning the muffins out of the tin and cooling them completely on a wire rack.

SWEETS

MEXICAN CANDIED
SWEET POTATOES

A popular Mexican street food, *camotes enmielados* are candied sweet potatoes that are spiked with *canela*—which lends it the cinnamon flavor of red hot candies—and raw, molassesy *piloncillo,* a form of unrefined cane sugar. They are simultaneously tooth-achingly sweet and mouthwateringly delicious, and are excellent served on a Thanksgiving table or as a dessert with vanilla ice cream. Chewy and sweet, they're also a great replacement for bananas in a split.

SERVES 4 TO 6

1½ pounds small sweet potatoes (4 to 6), peeled

1 (8-ounce) cone piloncillo or 1 cup packed dark brown sugar

1 (3-inch) canela stick (Mexican cinnamon stick), broken into several pieces

TIPS: The combined flavors of piloncillo and canela are essential to this dish. Seek them out at any Mexican grocery or in the Latin section of supermarkets. Piloncillo is a rock-hard, cone-shaped dark brown sugar. Mexican canela is the curled bark of a tree unrelated to true Vietnamese cinnamon.

1 Preheat the oven to 350°F.

2 Halve the sweet potatoes lengthwise, if needed, so they are no more than 1 inch wide. Arrange the sweet potatoes in a 2-quart baking dish and top with the piloncillo cone. Pour 1 cup water over the piloncillo, which will not fully dissolve, and scatter the pieces of canela around the pan. Tent with foil and place the baking dish on a large rimmed baking sheet.

3 Bake the sweet potatoes, basting every 20 to 30 minutes, until the piloncillo is melted and becomes a thick honey-like syrup and the sweet potatoes are tender and slightly shriveled on the outside, about 1½ hours. Remove from the oven and let cool. Remove and discard the canela pieces.

4 Serve the camotes with a spoonful of their syrup. The camotes will keep in an airtight container in the refrigerator, in their syrup, for 1 week.

PUDDING PIE

Good ol' black-bottom pudding pie: Make one batch of pudding, then divide it and mix in two different flavors, here chocolate and sweet potato. Layer it all in a gingersnap crust (although you can cheat with a store-bought chocolate or graham cracker crust) and top with whipped cream. This pie is just the thing to amp up your Thanksgiving spread.

MAKES ONE 9-INCH PIE

1½ cups finely crushed gingersnap cookies

¼ teaspoon kosher salt

3 tablespoons unsalted butter, melted

2 large egg yolks

½ cup sugar

1 cup whole milk

2 tablespoons cornstarch

4 ounces cream cheese, at room temperature

2 tablespoons dark rum

4 ounces bittersweet chocolate, melted

1 cup Sweet Potato Puree (page 25)

2 cups whipped cream

1 Preheat the oven to 350°F.

2 Dump the gingersnap crumbs and salt into a 9-inch pie plate. Drizzle the melted butter over the crumbs; then use a fork to work the butter into the crumbs until they are uniformly moist. Use the bottom of a glass or the back of a large spoon to pack the crumbs onto the bottom and sides of the pie plate. Bake the crust until firm, about 8 minutes. Remove from the oven and let cool.

3 In a heatproof bowl, whisk together the egg yolks and ¼ cup of the sugar.

4 In a small saucepan set over medium-high heat, whisk together the remaining ¼ cup sugar, the milk, and cornstarch. Cook, whisking constantly, until the mixture bubbles and thickens, 3 to 4 minutes. Remove the pan from the heat and, while whisking, gradually pour half of the thickened milk into the egg yolk mixture. Pour the yolk mixture into the saucepan with the remaining milk and whisk to combine. Set the pan over medium heat and cook, whisking constantly, until the pudding boils and becomes very thick, about 2 minutes. Remove the pan from the heat and stir in the cream cheese and rum.

5 Place the chocolate in a small bowl and add ¾ cup of the pudding base. Stir until the mixture is smooth. Pour the chocolate pudding into the pie shell and chill until set, about 1 hour.

6 Meanwhile, stir the sweet potato puree into the remaining pudding base. Cover and chill until the chocolate layer of the pie is set; then gently spread the sweet potato pudding over the chocolate layer. Cover loosely with plastic wrap and refrigerate for at least 3 hours and preferably overnight.

7 Top with whipped cream just before serving.

SWEET POTATO
ICE CREAM

Rich and smooth, this ice cream starts with cooking the sweet potato in milk, which helps prevent ice crystals from forming when the custard freezes. The ice cream base comes together in a snap, and while cashews are optional, they are delicious with the honey and cardamom. Serve this in a sundae with hot fudge, or make a "sweet potato pie" by spooning the ice cream into a graham cracker crust. Either way, top with toasted marshmallow crème.

MAKES ABOUT 1 QUART

ICE CREAM BASE

1 medium sweet potato (about ½ pound), peeled and chopped

1 cup whole milk

2 cups heavy cream

½ cup honey

½ cup packed light brown sugar

1 teaspoon vanilla extract

½ teaspoon kosher salt

½ teaspoon ground cardamom (optional)

Hot fudge

½ cup toasted, chopped cashews (optional)

Marshmallow crème

Maraschino cherries

1 **Make the ice cream base:** Combine the sweet potato, milk, and cream in a medium saucepan. Set over medium heat and bring to a simmer. Cook until the sweet potato is very tender, about 15 minutes. Pour the mixture into a blender and add the honey, brown sugar, vanilla, salt, and cardamom, if using. Process until very smooth, about 30 seconds. Refrigerate the ice cream base until it is very cold and there are no visible bubbles in it, at least 4 hours but preferably overnight.

2 Churn the ice cream in an ice cream maker according to the manufacturer's instructions.

3 When the ice cream is frozen, scoop it into a loaf pan and smooth the surface. Cover with plastic wrap and freeze until solid, at least 2 hours.

4 With a warmed scoop, dip scoops of ice cream into serving dishes. Top with hot fudge, cashews, and marshmallow crème and toast with a kitchen torch. Finish with a cherry.

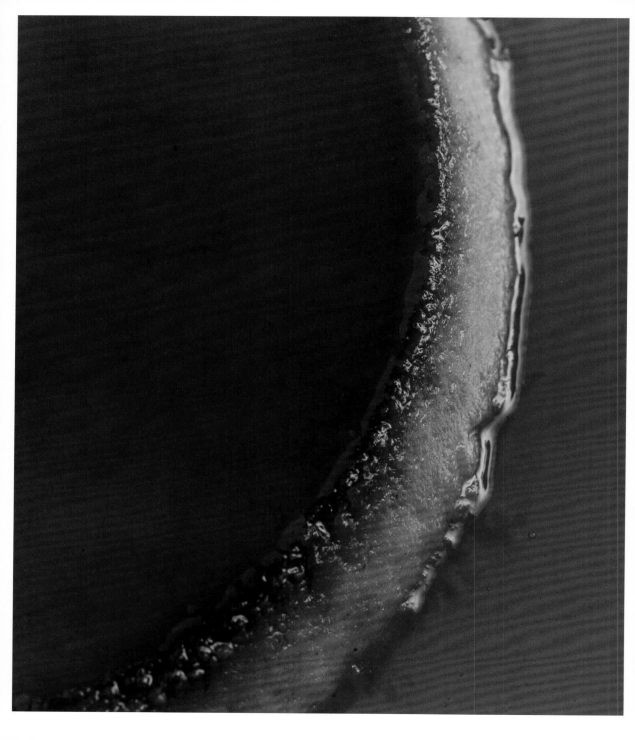

SWEET POTATO AND
SHERRY FLAN

This recipe came from my sister's in-laws, who live on a ranch outside of Puebla, Mexico. A large midday meal is prepared for the entire ranch staff every day, and this is a favorite dessert of theirs—and mine. It makes an elegant end to a meal; just don't feel like you have to tell your guests how easy it is to prepare.

SERVES 8

¾ cup sugar

3 large eggs

2 cups Sweet Potato Puree (page 25)

1 (15-ounce) can sweetened condensed milk

2 tablespoons dry sherry

½ teaspoon ground cinnamon

1 Preheat the oven to 325°F. Place a 9-inch pie plate in a 12-inch baking dish or ovenproof skillet.

2 Set a 10-inch skillet over medium heat. Sprinkle about 1 tablespoon of the sugar all over the bottom of the pan and let it melt, which will take between 10 and 20 seconds. Very gradually sprinkle more sugar onto the melted sugar, keeping pace with how fast it melts, until all the sugar has been added and melted. Let the sugar bubble while gently swirling the pan to incorporate areas that brown at different rates. When the caramel emits its first wisp of smoke, after 4 to 5 minutes total, carefully and quickly pour the caramel into the pie plate. Let the caramel harden.

3 In a large bowl, whisk together the eggs, sweet potato, sweetened condensed milk, sherry, and cinnamon. Pour the batter over the hardened caramel. Pour enough hot water into the baking dish to come halfway up the sides of the pie plate. Bake until the custard is set, about 1 hour. Remove the flan from the oven and let cool to room temperature. Refrigerate until ready to serve.

4 Run a knife around the edge of the flan and then invert it onto a large rimmed plate or platter. Cut into wedges and serve.

AMBROSIA
SWISS ROLL

SERVES 8

CAKE

Nonstick cooking spray

¾ cup all-purpose flour

½ teaspoon baking powder

½ teaspoon baking soda

¼ teaspoon kosher salt

3 large eggs

¾ cup granulated sugar

¾ cup Sweet Potato Puree
(page 25)

½ teaspoon grated orange zest

2 tablespoons confectioners'
sugar

FILLING

1 cup heavy cream

¼ cup confectioners' sugar

½ cup sour cream

1 cup finely chopped pineapple

GLAZE

2 cups confectioners' sugar

¼ cup orange juice

½ cup unsweetened coconut
flakes

This sponge cake is soft and light. It would be great with a layer of raspberry jam and whipped cream, but it's next-level delicious with this fresh take on ambrosia, a Southern salad of oranges, pineapple, and coconut. Sweet potatoes keep the sponge moist and balance the sweet fruit filling with a subtle earthiness.

1 Preheat the oven to 375°F. Spray an 18 × 13-inch rimmed baking sheet with cooking spray. Line it with a sheet of parchment and then spray the parchment.

2 **Make the cake:** In a small bowl, whisk together the flour, baking powder, baking soda, and salt.

3 In a large bowl or the bowl of a stand mixer, beat the eggs and granulated sugar until pale and thick, about 2 minutes. Add the sweet potato puree and orange zest and beat until fully combined. Add the dry ingredients and beat on low speed just to combine. The batter should be smooth and glossy, and pour like a ribbon into the prepared baking sheet. Smooth the top of the batter with an offset spatula, making sure to fill the corners, and then rap the pan on the counter several times to release any large air bubbles. Bake the cake until it springs back when touched and a cake tester inserted in the center comes out clean, about 14 minutes.

4 Meanwhile, lay a sheet of parchment paper on a baking sheet and sift the confectioners' sugar all over the parchment. Remove the baked cake from the oven and run a knife around the edges of the pan. Invert the cake onto the sugar-dusted parchment, remove the pan, and peel

off the top parchment. Fold one short edge of the parchment over a short edge of the cake, and then begin rolling the cake and parchment into a tight coil. Arrange a rack inside the baking sheet and set the cake on the rack with the seam facing down, so the cake does not spring to life and unroll itself. Let it cool.

5 **Meanwhile, make the filling:** In a medium bowl, whip the cream to soft peaks. Add the confectioners' sugar and whip to stiff peaks, about 30 seconds. Stir the sour cream into the whipped cream. Refrigerate until you're ready to fill the cake.

6 **Make the glaze:** Put the confectioners' sugar in a bowl, add the orange juice, and stir until all of the sugar is dissolved and the glaze is smooth and pourable.

7 Assemble the cake: Unroll the cake on a work surface, leaving the parchment underneath. Spread the cake with the filling, leaving a 1-inch border at one short end, and a $\frac{1}{2}$-inch border along the other three sides. Drain the pineapple of any pooled juice and evenly distribute the pineapple over the filling. Roll up the cake, starting at the short end with the $\frac{1}{2}$-inch border. Use the parchment to aid in the rolling—though don't forget it inside the cake! Return the rolled cake, seam-side down, to the rack and pour the glaze all over the cake, coating it in a thin layer. Immediately sprinkle the coconut onto the cake so it adheres to the glaze. Transfer the cake on the rack to the refrigerator and chill for at least 30 minutes; the cake is best after about 4 hours of chilling. If you plan to serve it the next day, refrain from glazing the cake until 1 hour before serving.

SUMMER
FRUIT COBBLER

This sweet potato cake batter is enriched with almond flour, which offers a nutty flavor and a pleasant texture. Using several types of fruit for a cobbler lends nuance to the wholesome dessert.

SERVES 6 TO 8

2 cups hulled and halved strawberries

2 cups raspberries

2 cups blackberries

2 cups chopped ripe peaches, apricots, or nectarines

¾ cup plus 1 tablespoon sugar

1 tablespoon cornstarch

1 cup all-purpose flour

½ cup almond flour

2 teaspoons baking powder

½ teaspoon kosher salt

6 tablespoons (¾ stick) unsalted butter, at room temperature

1 large egg

¾ cup Sweet Potato Puree (page 25)

2 teaspoons grated lemon zest

1 Arrange a rack in the lower third of the oven and preheat it to 350°F.

2 Toss the strawberries, raspberries, blackberries, and stone fruit in a 13 × 9 × 2-inch baking dish. In a small bowl, stir together ½ cup of the sugar and the cornstarch until the mixture is well blended. This simple act will ensure that the cornstarch is distributed evenly and gently thickens the fruit juices. Sprinkle the sugar mixture over the fruit, then toss it again to coat the fruit evenly. Let sit while you make the batter.

3 In a small bowl, stir together the flour, almond flour, baking powder, and salt. In a large bowl, beat the butter and ¼ cup of the sugar until pale and fluffy, about 2 minutes. Add the egg and beat to combine it fully; then beat in the sweet potato puree and lemon zest. Add the dry ingredients, beating just to incorporate and form a stiff batter. Drop 6 to 8 heaping tablespoonfuls of the batter evenly over the fruit. Sprinkle the batter with the remaining 1 tablespoon sugar. Set the cobbler on a rimmed baking sheet.

4 Bake the cobbler until the center is bubbly and the cake is risen and golden, 30 to 35 minutes. Let cool for at least 30 minutes before serving.

TIP: You can also make small tea cakes with this batter and a couple cups of whatever fresh berries are in season. Divide the batter among 12 greased standard muffin cups and top each with a few berries. Bake at 350°F for 20 to 25 minutes.

TRAIL MIX COOKIES

MAKES 24 COOKIES

1 cup peeled and grated sweet potato

1 cup all-purpose flour

½ cup (1 stick) unsalted butter, at room temperature

½ cup packed light brown sugar

½ cup granulated sugar

2 large eggs

1 teaspoon vanilla extract

½ teaspoon baking soda

½ teaspoon baking powder

½ teaspoon kosher salt

¾ cup quick-cooking oats

½ cup pecan pieces

½ cup dried cherries

½ cup semisweet chocolate chips

TIP: The cookie dough can be refrigerated for 1 day or shaped and frozen for 1 month.

These cookies are of the crispy-edged, chewy-centered variety. Sneaking a bit of grated sweet potato and quick-cooking oats into the batter means they are more wholesome than standard chocolate chip cookies, and the cherries and pecans make them right at home in a Christmas cookie swap. Make a double batch; they tend to vanish from the cooling rack. And try making sandwiches with them, using the icing from Ultimate Cream Cheese Cinnamon Rolls (page 117) as a filling.

1 Toss the sweet potato and flour in a small bowl. In a large bowl or the bowl of a stand mixer, beat the butter and sugars on medium speed until the mixture is a few shades paler and fluffy, about 2 minutes. Add the eggs and beat to fully combine, and then beat in the vanilla. Add the floured sweet potato, baking soda, baking powder, and salt, and mix on low speed until combined. Add the oats, pecans, cherries, and chocolate chips. Cover and chill the dough for at least 1 hour.

2 Preheat the oven to 375°F. Line 2 baking sheets with parchment paper.

3 Drop heaping tablespoons of the dough, spaced 1 inch apart, on the prepared baking sheets.

4 Bake until the cookies are browned around the edges and golden on top, 12 to 15 minutes. Transfer to a rack to cool. The cookies will keep in an airtight container for 3 days.

ACKNOWLEDGMENTS

Thanks to all the editors I have had the pleasure of working with and learning from over the years: Hunter Lewis, who hired me out of culinary school to work in the kitchens at *Saveur* and *Bon Appétit*; the whole editorial team at *Lucky Peach,* especially Peter Meehan, who has elevated recipe writing to an art form; and Ashley Meyer, who lassoed me into this project and has thoughtfully and gently steered me through the cookbook writing process.

To my parents, Bill and Katy, whose love, support, and stocked pantry encouraged me to tinker with food as a kid and to pursue a career in cooking. To my brother, Lou, the best kitchen assistant and eating buddy a girl could ask for, and to my sisters, Madeleine and Juliana, who helped taste, test, and critique these dishes.

To the Gorham-Sherlock clan, for their hospitality, generosity, and willingness to eat sweet potatoes everyday.

To those who contributed recipes, ideas, and sweet potato insights: Cara Chigazola and Ana Sortun, whose recipe from Oleana appears on the cover, Emily Toubali, Gerard Craft, Travis Flood, Hannah Clark, Betsy Rodriguez, Stuart Brioza, Malorie Sellers, Ashley Kemper, Andrea Nguyen, and Rachel Khong.

To Sarah Smith and David Black, for their guidance navigating the world of books.

To the team at Clarkson Potter for their hard work and creativity: Doris Cooper, Aaron Wehner, Todd Berman, Kevin Garcia, Cathy Hennessy, Stephanie Huntwork, Sonia Persad, Kathy Brock, Danielle Daitch, and Alexandria Martinez.

To the Smokey Roots: Kristin Teig, Catrine Kelty, and Joseph Ferraro, whose vibrant photography and styling bring these recipes to life.

And thanks most of all to my partner, Tiffany, who has eaten and critiqued every recipe in this book and still loves me and sweet potatoes. Your honesty, encouragement, and patience keep me focused on what really matters.

INDEX